D0061423

T H E
10
Most Important
Things You
Can Say to a
CATHOLIC

RON RHODES

HARVEST HOUSE PUBLISHERS
Eugene, Oregon 97402

Unless otherwise indicated, all Scripture quotations are taken from the New American Standard Bible ®, © 1960, 1962, 1963, 1968, 1971, 1972, 1973, 1975, 1977, 1995 by The Lockman Foundation. Used by permission.

Verses marked NIV are taken from the Holy Bible: New International Version®. NIV®. Copyright© 1973, 1978, 1984 by the International Bible Society. Used by permission of Zondervan Publishing House. The "NIV" and "New International Version" trademarks are registered in the United States Patent and Trademark Office by International Bible Society.

Cover by Terry Dugan Design, Minneapolis, Minnesota

The 10 Most Important Things Series by Ron Rhodes •

The 10 Most Important Things You Can Say to a Catholic

The 10 Most Important Things You Can Say to a Jehovah's Witness

The 10 Most Important Things You Can Say to a Mason

The 10 Most Important Things You Can Say to a Mormon

THE 10 MOST IMPORTANT THINGS YOU CAN SAY TO A CATHOLIC

Copyright © 2002 Ron Rhodes
Published by Harvest House Publishers
Eugene, Oregon 97402

Library of Congress Cataloging-in-Publication Data
Rhodes, Ron.
    The 10 most important things you can say to a Catholic / Ron Rhodes.
        p. cm. — (The 10 most important things series)
    Includes bibliographical references (p.).
    ISBN 0-7369-0537-5
        1. Catholic Church—Controversial literature. I. Title: Ten most important things you can say to a Catholic. II. Title.

BX1765.3 .R46 2002
282—dc21   2001038503

All rights reserved. No part of this publication may be reproduced, stored in a retrieval system, or transmitted in any form or by any means—electronic, mechanical, digital, photocopy, recording, or any other—except for brief quotations in printed reviews, without the prior permission of the publisher.

Printed in the United States of America.

02 03 04 05 06 07 / BP-MS / 10 9 8 7 6 5 4 3 2 1

This book is dedicated to the countless Christians across America who hold full-time jobs (often more than 40 hours per week), have families to take care of at home, and are very busy in life's various endeavors—yet still desire to become equipped to defend the truth of Christianity. May this little book assist you in reaching that worthy goal!

Acknowledgments

A special thanks to the staff at Harvest House Publishers for coming up with the idea for this concise book on witnessing to Roman Catholics. All of us agree there is a need for such a book. I also want to take this opportunity to thank those who have contacted me following the publication of my earlier book *Reasoning from the Scriptures with Catholics* (a considerably longer book—supplementary to the present volume—which is available in Christian bookstores). Your words of encouragement and your commitment to the cause of apologetics have been an inspiration to me.

Most of all, as always, I give a heartfelt thanks to my wife, Kerri, and my two children, David and Kylie, without whose support it would truly be impossible for me to do what I do.

Contents

If you run into witnessing trouble, feel free to contact Reasoning from the Scriptures Ministries. We will help you if we can.

Ron Rhodes
Reasoning from the Scriptures Ministries
P.O. Box 80087
Rancho Santa Margarita, CA 92688

www.ronrhodes.org

Free newsletter available upon request.

Ten Critical Points

This book is short by design. The chapters *in* this book are short by design. I believe there is much to be said for brevity. However—and I want to emphasize this very strongly—*brevity should not be thought of as "shallowness."* This book contains ten critical points to share with your Roman Catholic friends, but the points are concise and succinct. This book is intended to provide you with the most important apologetic information in the briefest possible fashion. In a day of information overload, the merits of such an approach seem obvious.

I devote an entire chapter to each of the ten most important points you can make to a Roman Catholic. Each chapter presents one primary point, and there are a number of supportive arguments in each chapter that substantiate that particular point. My desire is that you would become thoroughly equipped to theologically interact with your Roman Catholic friends, with a view to helping them understand the gospel of grace and bringing them into the kingdom of light—the kingdom of Jesus Christ (see Colossians 1:13,14).

It could be that the concise information in this book will cause you to want to go deeper and learn even more about interacting with Roman Catholics. That is a good thing. The more you learn, the more God can use you in witnessing. In such a case, I urge you to dig into my larger volume *Reasoning from the Scriptures with Catholics,* which is significantly more comprehensive than the book you are holding in your hands. You will find that these two books complement each other. For your convenience, at the end of each of the following chapters I provide relevant page numbers from *Reasoning from the Scriptures with Catholics.*

Icons Used in this Book

To make this guide easier to follow and understand, the icons below are used to highlight specific sections.

 The Roman Catholic Church's position on a particular doctrine.

 Key points to remember regarding the Roman Catholic position.

 The biblical position on a particular doctrine.

 An important point when refuting Roman Catholic theology or supporting biblical truth.

 A closer look at an important word, verse, or historical insight.

 A witnessing tip.

 Proceed with caution on a particular point.

 Quick-review checklist of apologetic points.

 Digging deeper—recomends supplementary reading from my book *Reasoning from the Scriptures with Catholics.*

1

The Apocryphal Books Are Helpful Historically,

But They Do Not Belong in the Bible

 One of the first things Protestants notice when interacting with Catholics is that the Catholic Bible is bigger. It has books the Protestant Bible does not have. These added books are collectively known as the Apocrypha. A key issue of debate between Protestants and Catholics is whether these books belong in the "canon" of Scripture.

The word *canon* comes from a Greek word meaning "measuring stick." Over time, the word came to be used metaphorically of books that were "measured" and thereby recognized as being God's Word. When we talk about the "canon of Scripture," we are referring to all the biblical books that collectively constitute God's Word.

Roman Catholics believe that the apocryphal books—seven complete books and four partial books, many of which originated in the period between the Old Testament and the New Testament—belong in the canon. While Protestants call these books "the Apocrypha," Roman Catholics prefer to refer to them as *deuterocanonical* (literally, "second canon"). This so-called "second canon," however, *does not* have secondary status among Roman Catholics. (For purposes of discussion, I will continue to refer to these books as the Apocrypha.)

The Roman Catholic Church decided these books belonged in the Bible shortly after the beginning of the Protestant Reformation. In fact, the Catholic Council of Trent (A.D. 1545–1563) canonized these books some 1500 years *after* they were written, largely as a reaction against the Protestant Reformation.

The Apocryphal Books

The Roman Catholic Apocrypha consists of Tobit, Judith, the Additions to Esther, the Additions to Daniel (the Prayer of Azariah and the Three Young Men, Susanna, and Bel and the Dragon), the Wisdom of Solomon, Ecclesiasticus (also called Sirach), Baruch (also called 1 Baruch), the Letter of Jeremiah, 1 Maccabees, and 2 Maccabees.

Martin Luther, the famous reformer, had criticized the Roman Catholic Church for not having scriptural support for such doctrines as praying for the dead. By canonizing the Apocrypha—which offers support for praying for the dead in 2 Maccabees 12:45-46—the Catholics then had "scriptural" support for this and other distinctively Catholic doctrines.[1]

Roman Catholics typically argue that, because the Septuagint (the Greek translation of the Hebrew Old Testament that predates the time of Christ) contains the Apocrypha, this must mean that the Apocrypha belongs in the canon. As well, church fathers such as Irenaeus, Tertullian, and Clement of Alexandria used the apocryphal books in public meetings of the church and accepted them as Scripture. Even the great theologian St. Augustine viewed these books as inspired.

Catholics also note that some early Christian catacomb scenes portray episodes from the Apocrypha, showing that the early Christian community was familiar with and used the Apocrypha. Moreover, the Council of Rome (A.D. 382), the Council of Hippo (A.D. 393), and the Council of Carthage (A.D. 397) accepted the Apocrypha. Finally, some apocryphal books were found in Qumran (the Dead Sea community) along with

Old Testament canonical books. (Collectively these documents have become known as the "Dead Sea Scrolls.")² These factors are said to prove that the apocryphal books belong in the canon.

The Apocrypha: The Roman Catholic View

- The Septuagint contains the Apocrypha.

- Some church fathers accepted the Apocrypha.

- Early catacomb scenes portray episodes from the Apocrypha.

- Some early church councils accepted the Apocrypha.

- Some apocryphal books were found at Qumran along with Old Testament canonical books.

The evidence indicates that the Apocrypha does not belong in the Bible. 1) History reveals that many church fathers denied the Apocrypha; 2) early Christian evidence argues against the Apocrypha; 3) the Palestinian Jews of the early Christian era rejected the Apocrypha; 4) the Apocrypha contains historical errors; 5) the Apocrypha contains unbiblical doctrines; 6) the Apocrypha was likely not in the earliest versions of the Septuagint; 7) scenes from the Apocrypha on Roman catacomb walls do not prove the Apocrypha's canonicity; 8) church councils are human institutions whose opinions sometimes reflect human fallibility; and 9) the presence of apocryphal books at Qumran (among the "Dead Sea Scrolls") does not prove their canonicity.

History reveals that many church fathers denied the Apocrypha. Though some church fathers spoke approvingly of the Apocrypha, others—notably Origen, Jerome, Athanasius, and Cyril of Jerusalem—denied its inspiration and canonicity. Therefore, merely quoting some church fathers in favor of the Apocrypha does not make a convincing argument. History reveals that some church fathers used apocryphal books for devotional or preaching purposes, but did not consider them canonical.³ One can demonstrate *respect* for a book without necessarily *canonizing* it.

 Unlike the New Testament books, which claim to be inspired (2 Timothy 3:16; 2 Peter 1:21; 1 Timothy 5:18; 2 Peter 3:16), none of the apocryphal books claim to be inspired. Further, no apocryphal book was written by a true prophet or apostle of God. And no apocryphal book was confirmed by divine miracles— something that happened often with the prophets in the Old Testament and apostles in the New Testament (for example, see 1 Kings 18 and Hebrews 2:4). Finally, no apocryphal book contains predictive prophecy, which would serve to confirm divine inspiration.⁴ Be sure to point these facts out to your Catholic friend.

Early Christian evidence argues against the Apocrypha. Though it is true that some early church leaders quoted several of the apocryphal books as Scripture (as Roman Catholics are quick to point out), it is also true that many early church leaders rejected these books. One of the earliest Christian lists of Old Testament books is that of Melito, the bishop of Sardis, who in A.D. 170 affirmed all the Old Testament books (except Esther), but did not mention a single apocryphal book. Moreover, in A.D. 367 the great champion of orthodoxy, Athanasius (a bishop of Alexandria), wrote his "paschal letter," in which he listed all the books of the New Testament, and all the Old Testament books except Esther. Although he did also mention some of the apocryphal books, such as the Wisdom of Solomon, the Wisdom of Sirach, Judith, and Tobit, he said these are "not indeed included in the Canon, but appointed by the Fathers to be read by those who newly join us, and who wish for instruction in the word of godliness."⁵

The Palestinian Jews of the early Christian era rejected the Apocrypha. The Jews of Palestine—including the Jewish Council of Jamnia, which met in A.D. 90—rejected the Apocrypha as Scripture. This is understandable, in view of the fact that there were no Jewish prophets who lived during the 400-year period between the Old and New Testaments. (It was during this time that much of the Apocrypha was written.) In keeping with this, ancient Jewish historian Flavius Josephus excluded the Apocrypha from Scripture. Philo, a Jewish teacher who lived in the first century, quoted from almost every canonical Old Testament book, but never once quoted from the Apocrypha.[6]

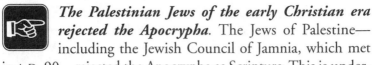 No New Testament writer quoted from any of the apocryphal books as Scripture or gave them the slightest authority as inspired books. Jesus and the disciples virtually ignored these books, something that would not have been the case if they had considered them to be inspired. By contrast, there are many quotations by Jesus and the apostles from the canonical books of the Old Testament. A good example of this is the Gospel of Matthew, which contains about 130 Old Testament citations and allusions.[7] Ask your Catholic friend about the significance of this.

 The Apocrypha contains historical errors. Scholars have noted that, unlike the canonical Scriptures, which have consistently proven to be historically accurate, the Apocrypha contains obvious historical and geographical errors. For example, Tobit contains historical errors—including the idea that Sennacherib was the son of Shalmaneser (1:15—he was actually the son of Sargon.) Second Maccabees likewise contains numerous discrepancies in chronological, historical, and numerical matters.

The reason this is significant is that historical and archaeo-logical studies have always been a friend to the canon of the Old and New Testaments, but not to the apocryphal books. While such studies have provided solid verification for numerous customs, places, names, and events mentioned in the Bible, this is not the case with the Apocrypha.

This does not mean the apocryphal books are worthless. They are valuable for historical purposes and cultural insights. But they are not inspired and do not belong in the canon. They are clearly man-made documents.

The Apocrypha contains unbiblical doctrines. Among these false doctrines is the doctrine of the Mass (2 Maccabees 12:42-45; contrast Hebrews 7:27); the notion that the world was created out of pre-existent matter (Wisdom of Solomon; contrast Genesis 1 and Psalm 33:9); the idea that giving alms and other works can make an atonement for sin (Ecclesiasticus 3:30; 3:3; 5:5; 20:28; 35:3; 45:16; 45:23; contrast Romans 3:20); the invocation and intercession of the saints (2 Maccabees 15:14; Baruch 3:4; contrast Matthew 6:9); the worship of angels (Tobit 12:12; contrast Colossians 2:18); and purgatory and the redemption of souls after death (2 Mac-cabees 12:42,46; contrast Hebrews 9:27).

Because we know that the Old and New Testaments are the Word of God, and because the Apocrypha contains doctrines that contradict the Old and New Testaments, we may conclude that the apocryphal books *are not* the Word of God. Why? Because *God does not contradict Himself.*

The Apocrypha was likely not in the earliest ver-sions of the Septuagint. It is true that late copies of the Septuagint include the Apocrypha. Scholars have noted, however, that although the Septuagint was translated several centuries *before* the time of Christ, it was apparently not until the fourth century *after* Christ that the Apocrypha was appended to this translation. Scholars know of no Septuagint manuscripts earlier than the fourth century that contain the Apocrypha, suggesting that the Apocrypha was not in the original Septuagint. But even if a first-century manuscript of the Septuagint were found with the Apocrypha in it, that still does not mean the Apocrypha belongs in the canon.

I say this because the apostles quoted from the first-century Septuagint in their New Testament writings—yet there is not a single quote from the Apocrypha in their writings. This could mean one of two things: 1) the Apocrypha was not in the first-century Septuagint (which is what the historical evidence seems to suggest), or 2) if the Apocrypha *was* in the first-century Septuagint, it was all but ignored by the apostles because they knew it did not truly belong in the canon of Scripture.

Scenes from the Apocrypha on Roman catacomb walls do not prove the Apocrypha's canonicity. The existence of such scenes simply indicates that some of the events recorded in apocryphal books were meaningful enough to some people that they drew pictures of them on the walls.[8] It is noteworthy that there are numerous events recorded in the Old and New Testament canonical books that are nowhere found on the catacomb walls, but this does not mean they are not canonical. Using reverse logic, the fact that certain scenes from the Apocrypha *are* recorded on catacomb walls does not mean that these books belong in the canon. This is faulty reasoning.

Church councils are human institutions whose opinions sometimes reflect human fallibility. The fact that some church councils accepted the Apocrypha may seem like a strong argument at first sight. But the fact that different church councils held during different time periods have come to differing conclusions on certain matters truly proves only one thing—*church councils are not infallible.* Only God and His

Word are infallible. Human beings and their councils make mistakes.

Furthermore, some of the councils—such as the local councils of Hippo and Carthage in North Africa—were heavily influenced by Augustine (A.D. 354–430), the most powerful voice of ancient times among those who accepted the Apocrypha. Augustine felt that the apocryphal books belonged in the Bible because of their mention "of extreme and wonderful suffering of certain martyrs"—but this is hardly a criteria for canonicity. Further, Augustine seems to have accepted the apocryphal books as canonical based largely on the fact that these books were contained in the Septuagint *of his day*. As noted above, though, there is good evidence to suggest that the original Septuagint did not contain the Apocrypha.[9]

Since the reasons for Augustine's acceptance of the Apocrypha are erroneous, the conclusions of the councils that drew many of their ideas from him are erroneous as well.

 The presence of apocryphal books at Qumran (among the "Dead Sea Scrolls") does not prove their canonicity. If the presence of a book at Qumran did prove its canonicity, this would mean that all the books discovered at Qumran (there were hundreds of books or fragments of books discovered) belong in the canon. The reality is that members of the Qumran community used many of these books for worship purposes without considering them canonical. There is no hard evidence that apocryphal books were venerated as Scripture among the Qumran inhabitants.

 There were five primary tests the early church used as it sought to formally recognize which books belonged in the canon: 1) *Was the book written or backed by a prophet or apostle of God?* (The Word of God, inspired by the *Spirit* of God for the *people* of God, must be communicated through a *man* of God.) 2) *Is the book authori-*

tative? (Does the book ring with the sense of "thus saith the Lord"?) 3) *Does the book tell the truth about God and doctrine as it is already known by previous revelation? 4) Does the book give evidence of having the power of God? 5) Was the book accepted by the people of God?*

Measuring the Apocrypha by these tests reveals that it does not belong in the canon. The books were not written by prophets or apostles of God. The books do not ring with the sense of "thus saith the Lord." The books contradict doctrines revealed in the pages of the Old and New Testaments. Though some church fathers used the books for devotional purposes, the books nevertheless fall far short of the transforming effect of the Old and New Testaments (as even many church fathers admitted), and hence do not display the power of God. And the books, for the most part, were not accepted on a broad scale by the people of God— at least not until 1500 years after their writing, when the Council of Trent pronounced them canonical.

Some Catholics may point to Hebrews 11:35— "Women received back their dead, raised to life again. Others were tortured and refused to be released, so that they might gain a better resurrection"(NIV)— and argue that this verse is a quotation from the Apocrypha (2 Maccabees 7:12). It is alleged that this proves the Apocrypha belongs in the Bible.

Such a view is incorrect for a number of reasons. First, even if Hebrews 11:35 *alludes* to an apocryphal book, it is definitely not a *quotation* of it. In fact, there is not a single clear quotation in the New Testament of any apocryphal book. This is not at all the case with the Old Testament books, for these books are quoted consistently throughout the New Testament.

Further, even if there were a citation of an apocryphal book in the New Testament, that in itself would not prove that the apocryphal book belongs in the canon of Scripture or that it is inspired by God. (It is noteworthy that the writer of 2 Maccabees *expressly disclaims inspiration.*[10]) Moreover, we must keep in mind that the Bible also alludes to pseudepigraphal books (*pseudepigrapha* = "false writings") like the Bodily Assumption of Moses (Jude 9), but even Roman Catholics reject that book from the canon. The Bible also quotes from pagan poets and philosophers (Acts 17:28; Titus 1:12), but that does not mean these writings are inspired or belong in the canon.

The Apocrypha Does Not Belong in the Bible

✓ Many church fathers denied the Apocrypha.

✓ Early Christian evidence argues against the Apocrypha.

✓ The Palestinian Jews of the early Christian era rejected the Apocrypha.

✓ The Apocrypha contains historical errors.

✓ The Apocrypha contains unbiblical doctrines.

✓ The Apocrypha was likely not in the earliest versions of the Septuagint.

✓ Scenes from the Apocrypha on Roman catacomb walls do not prove the Apocrypha's canonicity.

✓ Church councils are human institutions whose opinions sometimes reflect human fallibility.

✓ The presence of apocryphal books at Qumran (among the "Dead Sea Scrolls") does not prove their canonicity.

For further information on whether the Apocrypha belongs in the Bible, I invite you to consult my book *Reasoning from the Scriptures with Catholics,* pages 31–45.

2

The Bible Alone Is Authoritative,

Not Tradition

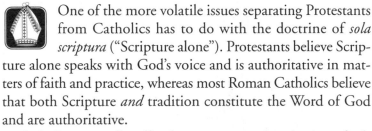 One of the more volatile issues separating Protestants from Catholics has to do with the doctrine of *sola scriptura* ("Scripture alone"). Protestants believe Scripture alone speaks with God's voice and is authoritative in matters of faith and practice, whereas most Roman Catholics believe that both Scripture *and* tradition constitute the Word of God and are authoritative.

Catholics generally offer three arguments in rejection of *sola scriptura* and in favor of the need for tradition:

1. *Not even the Bible argues for sola scriptura.* Catholic apologist Peter Kreeft said, "If we believe only what the Scripture teaches, we will not believe *sola scriptura*, for Scripture does not teach *sola scriptura*."[1] It is further argued that the early church did not even have the New Testament and depended on oral tradition. Since the early church was open to tradition, we also should be open to it.

2. *The Bible teaches the authority of tradition.* Catholics note that the apostle Paul wrote, "Brethren, stand firm and hold to the traditions which you were taught, whether by word of mouth or by letter from us" (2 Thessalonians 2:15). He also wrote,

"We command you, brethren, in the name of our Lord Jesus Christ, that you keep away from every brother who leads an unruly life and not according to the tradition which you received from us" (2 Thessalonians 3:6). It is further argued that the apostle John actually preferred oral tradition: "I had many things to write to you, but I am not willing to write them to you with pen and ink" (3 John 13).

Circular Argument

Some Catholics argue *for* tradition based on what they have learned *from* tradition. This is arguing in a circle: "We know tradition is true because tradition tells us so."

---

3. *The Bible cannot be correctly interpreted without tradition.* Catholics say tradition is for the highest good of the church, because without it, we end up with division (multiple denominations), which is an "intolerable scandal" in view of the fact that Christ called the church to unity. The Bible *alone* (without tradition) is not "a safe guide as to what we are to believe."[2]

The Bible Versus Tradition: The Roman Catholic View

- Not even the Bible argues for *sola scriptura.*
- The Bible teaches the authority of tradition.
- The Bible cannot be correctly interpreted without tradition.

 The Bible alone is authoritative. 1) Tradition is to be respected but not exalted; 2) only the Bible is inspired; 3) an explicit statement of *sola scriptura* in the Bible is not necessary; 4) all apostolic tradition in regard to faith and practice is recorded in the New Testament; 5) Rome's claim that the Bible cannot be interpreted apart from tradition contains a fatal flaw; 6) Scripture sets parameters beyond which we are not free to go; and 7) the Bible verses Catholics cite in favor of tradition are misinterpreted.

 Tradition is to be respected but not exalted. Christians who hold to *sola scriptura* do not say there never was a time when God's Word was spoken. Obviously there was such a time. But the teachings and traditions once communicated orally by the apostles were committed by them to writing for all generations to come. All that God intends us to have is found within the Scriptures.

That is not to say that tradition is worthless. "Tradition" in the form of church confessions and council pronouncements should be respected, but such tradition is not "apostolic," is not God's revelation, and does not have an authority equal to that of Scripture.

 Only the Bible is inspired. The biblical Greek word for inspiration *(theopneustos)* literally means "God-breathed." In 2 Timothy 3:16 we read that "all Scripture is God-breathed"(NIV). The Greek form here of this word indicates that the Bible is the result of the "breath of God." Because Scripture is breathed out by God—because it originates from Him—it is true and inerrant.

Biblical inspiration may be defined as God's superintending of the human authors so that, using their own individual personalities—and even their writing styles—they composed and recorded *without error* His revelation to humankind in the words of the original biblical manuscripts. The Bible is thus authoritative.

Second Peter 1:21 provides a key insight regarding the human–divine interchange in the process of inspiration. This verse informs us that "prophecy [or Scripture] never had its origin in the will of man, but men spoke from God as they were carried along by the Holy Spirit" (NIV). The phrase "carried along" literally means "forcefully borne along."

Even though human beings were used in the process of writing down God's Word, they were all literally "borne along" by the Holy Spirit. The human wills of the authors were not the originators of God's message. God did not permit the will of sinful human beings to misdirect or erroneously record His message. Rather, as Norman Geisler and William Nix put it, "God *moved* and the prophet *mouthed* these truths; God *revealed* and man *recorded* His word."[3]

 Jesus rebuked some of the Pharisees thus: "Neglecting the commandment of God, you hold to the tradition of men" (Mark 7:8). Likewise, in Colossians 2:8 the apostle Paul warns: "See to it that no one takes you captive through philosophy and empty deception, *according to the tradition of men,* according to the elementary principles of the world, rather than according to Christ" (emphasis added). Any tradition that conflicts with Scripture is to be rejected. Be sure to share these verses with your Catholic friend.

 Many Catholics argue that the Roman Catholic church *gave* us the Bible, and hence it is authoritative *over* the Bible. This simply is not true. The canon of Scripture began to form in the very days the Bible was being written, before the Roman Catholic Church was even in existence. Luke's Gospel was recognized as Scripture *within a few years of its writing* (1 Timothy 5:18 quotes Luke 10:7 as Scripture). Paul's writings were also recognized as Scripture *during his own day* (2 Peter 3:16; 1 Corinthians 14:37; 1 Thessalonians 2:13). Besides, it is God who *determines* the canon; human beings merely *discover* the canon.[4]

As F.F. Bruce put it, the New Testament canon was not demarcated by the arbitrary decree of a council: "When at last a Church Council—the Synod of Carthage in A.D. 397—listed the 27 books of the New Testament, it did not confer upon them any authority which they did not already possess, but simply recorded their previously established canonicity."[5]

 An explicit statement of* sola scriptura *in the Bible is not necessary. A doctrine does not have to be taught explicitly in Scripture in order for that doctrine to be recognized as true. The doctrine of the Trinity is an example. Scripture does not come right out and say, "God is a Trinity." But the Bible does implicitly teach this doctrine by telling us that 1) there is one God (Deuteronomy 6:4), and 2) the Father, the Son, and the Holy Spirit are distinct persons who are God (Matthew 3:16,17; 28:19). Likewise, although the doctrine of *sola scriptura* may not be explicitly taught in Scripture, it is implicitly taught.[6]

The Lord Jesus, for example, used Scripture as His final court of appeal. Jesus affirmed that "Scripture cannot be broken" (John 10:35). To the devil, Jesus consistently responded, "It is written..." (Matthew 4:4-10). Jesus affirmed the Bible's divine inspiration (Matthew 22:43), indestructibility (Matthew 5:17-18), infallibility (John 10:35), final authority (Matthew 4:4,7,10), historicity (Matthew 12:40; 24:37), scientific accuracy (Matthew 19:2-5), and factual inerrancy (John 17:17; Matthew 22:29).

The apostle Paul also affirmed the full adequacy of Scripture in 2 Timothy 3:16,17: "All Scripture is inspired by God and profitable for teaching, for reproof, for correction, for training in righteousness; that the man of God may be adequate, equipped for every good work." The context for understanding the full significance of this passage is verse 15, where Paul tells Timothy that "from childhood you have known the sacred writings *which are able to give you the wisdom that leads to salvation* through faith which is in Christ Jesus" (emphasis added). Jewish boys began formally studying the Old Testament when they were five years of age. Timothy had been taught Scripture by his mother and grandmother beginning at this age. Verse 15 thus indicates that the *Scriptures alone* are sufficient to provide the necessary wisdom that leads to salvation through faith in Christ. The Scriptures alone are the source of spiritual knowledge.

 Jesus, in the Gospel of Matthew, told the Pharisees and teachers of the law: "You invalidated the word of God for the sake of your tradition" (Matthew 15:6). There is no doubt that Jesus placed Scripture *above* tradition, and indicated that tradition can lead people astray. Emphasize this point to your Catholic friend.

 All apostolic tradition in regard to faith and practice is recorded in the New Testament. This does not mean that almost everything Jesus or the apostles said is in the New Testament (see John 20:30; 21:25). But all the apostolic teaching God wanted communicated to His people necessary for faith and practice is found in the New Testament (see 2 Timothy 3:15-17).

The Bible itself reveals it was God's will for His revelations to be written down and preserved for coming generations. "Moses wrote down all the words of the LORD" (Exodus 24:4). Joshua too "wrote these words in the book of the law of God" (Joshua 24:26). Samuel "told the people the ordinances of the kingdom, and wrote them in the book and placed it before the LORD" (1 Samuel 10:25). The Lord instructed Isaiah, "Take for yourself a large tablet and write on it in ordinary letters..." (Isaiah 8:1). What the apostle Paul wrote was at "the Lord's command" (1 Corinthians 14:37). The apostle John was commanded by the Lord to "write, therefore, what you have seen" (Revelation 1:19 NIV).

Rome's claim that the Bible cannot be interpreted apart from tradition contains a fatal flaw. The big problem is that once Rome gives a definitive explanation of a Bible passage via tradition, Rome's explanation must then be interpreted—and in many cases Rome's explanations are more complicated than the Bible passage.[7]

So Rome has just pushed the problem back one generation. Now, instead of needing help interpreting the Bible, we need help interpreting the tradition that is supposed to make the Bible clearer.

Protestants believe the Bible is *sufficiently* clear. This is a doctrine called *perspicuity*. This does not mean that every single verse in the Bible is equally clear or easy to understand. But it does mean that the main teachings of the Bible are clear.

 Church history reveals there are contradictions in the many traditions of Rome. Abelard (A.D. 1079–1142) recognized hundreds of such contradictions. For example, some church authorities accepted the Immaculate Conception of Mary, while others did not.[8] This means that *tradition is not infallible,* nor is it authoritative. Point this out to your Catholic acquaintance.

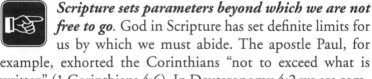 ***Scripture sets parameters beyond which we are not free to go.*** God in Scripture has set definite limits for us by which we must abide. The apostle Paul, for example, exhorted the Corinthians "not to exceed what is written" (1 Corinthians 4:6). In Deuteronomy 4:2 we are commanded: "You shall not add to the word which I am commanding you, nor take away from it, that you may keep the commandments of the LORD your God which I command you." Proverbs 30:5,6 instructs us: "Every word of God is tested; He is a shield to those who take refuge in Him. Do not add to

His words or He will reprove you, and you will be proved a liar." Revelation 22:18-19 likewise tells us: "I testify to everyone who hears the words of the prophecy of this book: if anyone adds to them, God will add to him the plagues which are written in this book; and if anyone takes away from the words of the book of this prophecy, God will take away his part from the tree of life and from the holy city, which are written in this . book."

The Roman Catholic exaltation of tradition violates the intent and spirit of these commandments. It is not wrong to respect tradition, but it is wrong to attribute the same authority to tradition that is attributed to Scripture. One has its source in man, the other in God.

 The Bible verses Roman Catholics cite in favor of tradition are misinterpreted. Among these verses are Matthew 2:23; John 21:25; 2 Thessalonians 2:15; 2 Thessalonians 3:6; and 3 John 13.

Matthew 2:23. In this passage we read that Jesus "came and lived in a city called Nazareth. This was to fulfill what was spoken through the prophets: 'He shall be called a Nazarene.'" Catholics argue that this statement is not found in any Old Testament verse, but is nevertheless said to have come from the prophets. That can only mean one thing—it must have been passed down from generation to generation through oral tradition.

In response, it is a tremendous leap in logic to go from an undocumented prophetic quote to the existence of a supposed oral tradition for which there is almost no historical evidence. Many scholars believe that the primary meaning of Jesus being called a "Nazarene" has to do with His despised character. In biblical times Nazareth was considered a place of vice. This prompted Nathaniel to say, "Can any good thing come out of Nazareth?" (John 1:46). In view of this, being called a

"Nazarene" back in those days was considered scornful and amounted to being called a *despised person.*

It may be that Matthew was not intending to communicate that a particular Old Testament prophet foretold that the Messiah would live in Nazareth, but rather that the Old Testament prophets *collectively* foretold that He would be a despised character (Psalm 69:8,20,21; Isaiah 11:1; 49:7; 53:2-8). Matthew certainly emphasizes this theme in his Gospel (Matthew 8:20; 11:16-19; 15:7,8). Seen then in this light, Matthew is giving us the substance of a number of Old Testament prophets, not a direct quotation from a single prophet.[9] Note that Matthew made reference to "prophets" (plural), which would seem to indicate that he was drawing his information from more than one prophet.

John 21:25. In this verse we are told the following: "There are also many other things which Jesus did, which if they were written in detail, I suppose that even the world itself would not contain the books that would be written." Catholics thus argue that the New Testament is incomplete and there is clearly a need for tradition.

John's only point in this verse is that Jesus' ministry was so wonderful, so miraculous, so beyond the ability of human words to fully capture, that the Gospel account he wrote reflects *only a portion* of the wonder of our divine Lord. John's sense is that he had but dipped a cup in the ocean of wonder that is Jesus Christ. Someone has calculated that one can read the accounts of Jesus in the Gospels in about three hours. If we consider all that Jesus said and did during His full three-year ministry, then surely John's expression is reasonable.

 Since John's Gospel was directly inspired by the Holy Spirit, we know for certain that what is communicated in this Gospel is *exactly what God wanted to be*

communicated. Sola scriptura does not claim that what
is in the Bible is *exhaustive*, it only claims that what is
in the Bible is *fully sufficient*. Everything that God
wanted us humans to have in terms of His revelation
to us is found within Scripture. To cite John 21:25 in
support of tradition is thus unwarranted.

Second Thessalonians 2:15. Here Paul says, "Brethren, stand
firm and hold to the traditions which you were taught, whether
by word of mouth or by letter from us." Catholics cite this verse
to show that the apostle Paul believed in the authority of tradition.

At first sight, this verse might seem to support the Catholic
position. But notice the critically important words, "from *us*"
(that is, *the apostles*). Paul was talking to people he had personally taught as an apostle of God.

The Greek word for "traditions" *(paradosis)* refers to *that
which has been passed down.* Paul had earlier passed down some
apostolic teachings about the second coming of Christ to the
Thessalonian Christians (the context of 2 Thessalonians 2
makes this clear), and Paul reminds them in this verse to hold
firm to those teachings.[10]

The apostles for a time communicated their teachings *orally*
until those teachings could be permanently recorded in *written*
form. Once the apostles committed their teachings to written
form, and then died, the written Scriptures alone became our
final authority for matters of faith and practice (2 Timothy
3:15-17). (If the Catholic to whom you are speaking argues that
the Catholic bishops are the successors of the apostles, see
chapter 4.)

Second Thessalonians 3:6. In this verse we read, "We command you, brethren, in the name of our Lord Jesus Christ, that
you keep away from every brother who leads an unruly life and
not according to the tradition which you received from us."

Catholics cite this verse in support of the authority of tradition.[11]

"Tradition" (again, *paradosis*) here refers to what the apostle Paul had orally passed down to the Thessalonian believers—that is, teaching directly from the mouth of an apostle. In context, the "tradition" of which Paul speaks relates to the importance of living a productive and disciplined life, instead of living in an unruly way (see verses 7-15). Eventually, this oral teaching was committed to writing, and the oral teaching was rendered obsolete. There was no further need for oral tradition.

Third John 13. In this verse John writes, "I had many things to write to you, but I am not willing to write them to you with pen and ink." Catholics argue from this verse that John much preferred oral tradition to written Scripture.[12] But all John was doing was expressing his desire to have personal contact with his readers as opposed to just writing them a letter. Indeed, that is what John says in the very next verse: "I hope to see you shortly, and we will speak face to face" (3 John 14).

The Bible Alone Is Authoritative, Not Tradition

✓ Tradition is to be respected but not exalted.

✓ Only the Bible is inspired.

✓ An explicit statement of *sola scriptura* in the Bible is not necessary.

✓ All apostolic tradition in regard to faith and practice is recorded in the New Testament.

✓ The claim that the Bible cannot be interpreted apart from tradition contains a fatal flaw.

✓ Scripture sets parameters beyond which we are not free to go.

✓ The Bible verses Roman Catholics cite in favor of tradition are misinterpreted.

For further information on the Catholic view of *sola scriptura* and tradition, consult *Reasoning from the Scriptures with Catholics,* pages 47–83.

Peter Was a Great Apostle,

But He Was Not the First Pope

Roman Catholics allege that St. Peter's Basilica in Vatican City was built above Peter's tomb. They believe that Peter took up residence in Rome in A.D. 42 and remained there until his martyrdom in A.D. 67. Peter was reportedly the first bishop, or pope, of Rome, ruling the universal church from that city. Whoever succeeds Peter as the bishop of Rome also succeeds him as pope.

There are a handful of New Testament passages that Catholics cite in support of the idea that Peter attained supremacy in the early church and became the first pope. For example, Peter's name appears first in various lists of the apostles (see Matthew 10:2-4; Mark 3:16-19; Luke 6:14-16). Further, Catholics believe Jesus called Peter the "rock" upon whom the church would be built (Matthew 16:18), allegedly indicating that Peter was being elevated to supremacy. We are also told that, because Jesus gave Peter the "keys of the kingdom" (Matthew 16:19), his primacy is evident. As well, when Jesus told Peter to "tend my sheep" (John 21:15-17), Jesus was obviously placing Peter in a position of authority over the church. And Jesus' prayer that

Peter's faith would not fail ensures Peter's infallibility (Luke 22:31,32).

Catholic scholars realize that Scripture nowhere explicitly states Peter went to Rome. But they argue that tradition on this point is unmistakable. Furthermore, they believe that in the light of this tradition, certain New Testament passages seem to confirm that Peter may have ended up in Rome.[1] For example, Acts 12:17 affirms that, following Peter's release from prison, "he left and went to another place." It is suggested that this other "place" was Rome.

Peter, the First Pope: The Roman Catholic View

- Peter's name appears first in various lists of the apostles.

- Jesus called Peter the "rock" upon whom the church would be built (Matthew 16:18).

- Jesus gave Peter the "keys of the kingdom" (Matthew 16:19).

- Jesus placed Peter in authority over the church, saying "tend my sheep" (John 21:15-17).

- Jesus prayed that Peter's faith would not fail, ensuring Peter's infallibility (Luke 22:31,32).

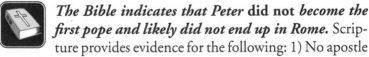

The Bible indicates that Peter* did not *become the first pope and likely did not end up in Rome. Scripture provides evidence for the following: 1) No apostle attained a supreme position in New Testament times; 2) no New Testament epistle teaches that Peter became pope; 3) Paul affirmed he was not inferior to *any* other apostle (including Peter); 4) the history of the early church in the book of Acts argues against the existence of a papacy; 5) Peter was not infallible; 6) Peter's name being listed first shows only his importance—

not his papacy; 7) the "rock" upon which the church would be built was not Peter but his *confession of faith* that Jesus is the Christ (Matthew 16:18); 8) the "keys of the kingdom" relate not to Peter's supremacy but to his privilege of preaching the gospel; 9) Jesus' prayer that Peter's faith would not fail relates only to Peter's restoration following his denial of Christ (Luke 22:31,32); 10) Jesus' instruction to "tend My sheep" was given not to elevate Peter over the other apostles but to bring him back up to their level; and 11) the claim that Peter ended up in Rome is problematic.

 No apostle attained a supreme position in New Testament times. All the New Testament verses that speak of Peter are virtually silent about any alleged supremacy on his part. If Peter became pope, wouldn't at least one Bible verse clearly say so?

 Just prior to Christ's arrest and crucifixion, some of the disciples got into an argument over who among them would be the greatest in the kingdom (Luke 22:24-30). Why would the disciples continue to ask this question if the issue had been settled, with Peter having emerged as God's choice for a supreme position?[2] The fact that such discussions took place shows that *no* apostle had attained a supreme position during Jesus' three-year ministry. Point this out to your Catholic friend.

 No New Testament epistle teaches that Peter became pope, nor is there any mention of a papacy. Instead, we find all the disciples working together on an apparently equal level of authority.

If Peter had attained a supreme position of power, he would likely have said something in his second epistle (2 Peter) to the

effect that his readers should be sure to follow his successor in
Rome.[3] After all, Peter was getting on in years, and would have
supported the papacy had such an institution existed. But Peter
did no such thing because there was no papacy.

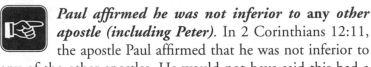 *Paul affirmed he was not inferior to* **any** *other* *apostle (including Peter).* In 2 Corinthians 12:11, the apostle Paul affirmed that he was not inferior to any of the other apostles. He would not have said this had a papacy been in existence. It is also highly revealing that while Peter is prominent in the first 12 chapters of the book of Acts, the apostle Paul is the prominent figure in chapters 13–28. This would not make sense if Peter had become the pope.

 When Paul lists the authority structure in the early church in 1 Corinthians 12:28, there is no mention of a pope: "God has appointed in the church, first apostles, second prophets, third teachers" (1 Corinthians 12:28).[4] Ask your Catholic friend: *Why the* *omission?*

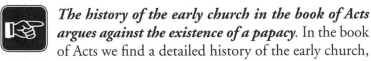 *The history of the early church in the book of Acts* *argues against the existence of a papacy.* In the book of Acts we find a detailed history of the early church, and there is not even a hint of the existence of a papacy or of Petrine supremacy. Instead we find verses that indicate Peter was *not* in a supreme position. Acts 8:14 says the apostles "sent" Peter and John to Samaria after they heard about God's work in Samaria. (Peter would have done the sending had he been supreme.) Further, Peter played no supreme role in the Jerusalem Council (see Acts 15:1-35), for he is portrayed as one among a number of apostles. James was apparently in charge of this council (see verses 13-35).

Peter was not infallible. In the book of Galatians, the apostle Paul provides us an example of Peter's obvious fallibility:

When Cephas [Peter] came to Antioch, I opposed him to his face, because he stood condemned. For prior to the coming of certain men from James, he used to eat with the Gentiles; but when they came, he began to withdraw and hold himself aloof, fearing the party of the circumcision. The rest of the Jews joined him in hypocrisy, with the result that even Barnabas was carried away by their hypocrisy. But when I saw that they were not straightforward about the truth of the gospel, I said to Cephas in the presence of all, "If you, being a Jew, live like the Gentiles and not like the Jews, how is it that you compel the Gentiles to live like Jews?" (Galatians 2:11-14).

Peter clearly was not immune from error. He made a mistake—*and in a matter of faith, at that.* Peter also shows an attitude of hypocrisy in his behavior, something hardly fitting for a "supreme pontiff."

If Peter had been a supreme pontiff during this time, Paul would have been completely out of order in publicly correcting Peter as he did (Galatians 2:11-14). Paul's correction shows quite clearly that Peter was not considered supreme. Ask your Catholic friend about this.

Peter's name being listed first shows only his importance—not his papacy. It is true that Peter's name often comes first in lists of the apostles (Matthew 10:2-4, Mark 3:16-19, Luke 6:14-16), but this does not mean Peter was supreme or became a pope. Peter certainly played a dominant role in the early church, and may have even become the spokesman and representative of the twelve during Jesus'

three-year ministry.[5] But he viewed himself as merely *one among many* who shepherded God's flock, referring to himself as a "fellow elder" (1 Peter 5:1). And, as noted previously, it was James who exercised primacy at the Council of Jerusalem, not Peter (Acts 15:1-35).

First and Second Peter

Some Catholics suggest that because Peter wrote two New Testament books, his role was central. But the apostle Paul wrote 13 books in the New Testament. The fact that Peter wrote a small portion of the New Testament is no indication of a rise to primacy.

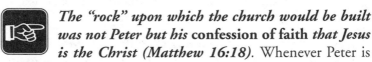

The "rock" upon which the church would be built was not Peter but his confession of faith *that Jesus is the Christ (Matthew 16:18).* Whenever Peter is referred to in Matthew 16, it is in the second person ("you"), but "this rock" is in the third person (verse 18). Moreover, "Peter" *(petros)* is a masculine singular term and "rock" *(petra)* is a feminine singular term. Hence, they do not seem to be referring to the same thing. Jesus did not say to Peter, "You are *Petros,* and upon this *Petros* I will build my church." Jesus said, "You are *Petros* (Peter), and upon this *petra* I will build my church." It would seem that, in context, *petra* refers to Peter's confession of faith that Jesus is the Christ.

This is supported by the fact that the context of Matthew 16:13-20 is all about Jesus, not Peter.[6] Indeed, the key issue of discussion is Jesus' identity. Jesus asked the disciples about who the people said He was (verse 13). Peter then declared correctly that Jesus was the Christ (verse 16). Then in verse 20, to prevent a premature disclosure of His identity, Jesus warned them not to tell anyone that He was the Christ. *Throughout this entire passage Jesus is the theme, not Peter.*

Catholics may respond that Jesus would have spoken these words to Peter in the Aramaic language: "You are *Kepha,* and upon this *kepha* I will build my church." Unlike the Greek, where two different word forms are used—*petros* and *petra,* the Aramaic expression would have used one word form *(kepha),* and hence Peter must be the "rock" of which Christ spoke.

All of this is mere conjecture. We do not know what Jesus might have said in the Aramaic. What we do have are Greek New Testament manuscripts that use two distinct words—*petros* and *petra.* And since Scripture is inspired by the Holy Spirit, the exact words God wanted in Matthew 16:18 were placed into this verse by divine superintendence.

 Ephesians 2:20 affirms that the church is "built on the foundation of the apostles and prophets, Christ Jesus Himself being the corner stone." Two things are clear from this: first, *all* the apostles, not just Peter, are the foundation of the church; second, the only one who is given a place of prominence is Christ, the corner stone. Peter himself referred to Christ as "the corner stone" of the church (1 Peter 2:7), and the rest of believers as "living stones" in the superstructure of the church (verse 4). Colossians 1:17,18 likewise affirms that Christ alone is the head of the church. Both the immediate context of Matthew 16:18 and the broader context of all of Scripture point away from Peter being "the rock." Help your Catholic friend understand that "no man can lay a foundation other than the one which is laid, which is Jesus Christ" (1 Corinthians 3:11).

 The "keys of the kingdom" relate not to Peter's supremacy but to his privilege of preaching the gospel. In Matthew 16:19 we read Jesus' words to

Peter: "I will give you the keys of the kingdom of heaven; whatever you bind on earth will be bound in heaven, and whatever you loose on earth will be loosed in heaven" (NIV). In the New Testament a key always implies authority to open a door and give entrance to a place or realm. Jesus, for example, possesses the keys of death and Hades, implying His authority to grant or deny access to these realms (Revelation 1:18).

Though Catholics argue that Jesus' gift of the keys of the kingdom to Peter indicates supreme authority, the context relates only to witnessing and evangelism by the apostles. This verse is teaching that the apostles were given the power to grant or deny access into the kingdom of God *based on how people responded to the gospel message.* Those who responded favorably to the gospel were "granted" access, while those who refuse to believe were "denied" access to the kingdom of God.

We know this to be true because the terms "bind" and "loose" were Jewish idioms that, in the present context, indicate that what is announced on earth has *already been determined in heaven.* To *bind* meant to forbid, refuse, or prohibit; to *loose* meant to permit or allow. We can announce the prohibition or allowance of certain things on earth because heaven (or God) has already made a pronouncement on these matters. "Binding" in the context of Matthew 16:19 refers to prohibiting entry into God's kingdom to those who reject the apostolic witness of Jesus Christ. "Loosing" refers to granting entry into God's kingdom to those who accept that witness (see John 20:23; Acts 2:38-41). The apostles could prohibit entry *(bind)* or grant entry *(loose)* into God's kingdom only because heaven had already declared that entry into the kingdom hinged on accepting their witness regarding Jesus Christ.

 In the book of Acts, it is clear that Peter and the other apostles did indeed "grant access" into the kingdom of God to various people. Jews (Acts 2:14-36),

Samaritans (8:4-25), and Gentiles (9:32–10:48) were granted access to the kingdom based on their positive response to the gospel. What we do *not* see in the book of Acts is Peter rising to a position of supremacy and exercising authority over all others.

Jesus' prayer that Peter's faith would not fail relates only to Peter's restoration following his denial of Christ. In Luke 22:31,32 we read Jesus' words to Peter: "Simon, Simon, behold, Satan has demanded permission to sift you like wheat; but I have prayed for you, that your faith may not fail; and you, when once you have turned again, strengthen your brothers." Though Catholic theologians argue that Jesus' prayer ensures Peter's infallibility as pope, the truth is that this passage relates only to Peter's restoration following his abysmal threefold denial of Christ (see Luke 22:34). There is nothing in the verse to even remotely suggest that Christ was making some veiled promise relating to Peter's infallibility. Jesus' prayer for Peter is in keeping with His general intercessory ministry for all believers (Romans 8:34; Hebrews 7:25; see also John 17:15).

Jesus' instruction to "tend My sheep" was given not to elevate Peter over the other apostles but to bring him back up to their level. Jesus exacts a threefold confession of love from Peter in John 21:15-17 to make up for his threefold denial. The Lord is simply restoring a fallen apostle. The only reason Peter was singled out here is that he is the only apostle who denied Christ.[7]

Elsewhere in Scripture we see that the other apostles are also called to feed and watch out for the "sheep" of the church (see Acts 20:28). This indicates that Peter was not given some unique calling apart from the other apostles. Peter himself wrote:

> Therefore, I exhort the elders among you, as your *fellow
> elder* and witness of the sufferings of Christ, and a par-
> taker also of the glory that is to be revealed, *shepherd the
> flock of God among you*, exercising oversight not under
> compulsion, but voluntarily, according to the will of God;
> and not for sordid gain, but with eagerness; nor yet as
> lording it over those allotted to your charge, but proving
> to be examples to the flock. And when the Chief Shep-
> herd appears, you will receive the unfading crown of glory
> (1 Peter 5:1-4, emphasis added).

Notice two things here: 1) Peter indicates that others beside himself shepherd the flock of God, thereby showing he is not unique; and 2) Peter refers to himself as a "fellow elder," thereby putting himself on the same level as others.

 ***The claim that Peter ended up in Rome is prob-
lematic.*** Peter ministered primarily among the Jews of his time (Galatians 2:7,8), so it would have been strange for him to move to Rome, since that city was not known as a center of Judaism. The first 15 chapters of the book of Acts show that Peter was in Jerusalem, Judea, Samaria, Galilee, and Antioch. There is never any mention of Rome.

It is highly revealing that the apostle Paul, in his epistle to the Romans (written about A.D. 58), greets some 26 people by name (see Romans 16:1-16), but *Peter is not one of them*. It seems inconceivable that Paul would have failed to give a greeting to Peter if Peter had indeed been headquartered in Rome (since A.D. 42, according to Catholics).

 In the epistles written by the apostle Paul while he was in prison in Rome—including Ephesians, Philippians, Colossians, and Philemon—there is *never* any mention of a visit from Peter. If Peter had been headquar-
tered in Rome, it would be unthinkable that he would not have visited Paul. It would also be unthinkable for

Peter to have visited him and Paul not to have mentioned it in one of the epistles (see 2 Timothy 4:16). Ask your Catholic friend about this.

Does Acts 12:17 indicate that Peter went to Rome, as Catholics claim? In this verse we read that, following Peter's release from prison, "he left and went to another place." Although Catholics suggest that Peter may have gone to Rome, he could just as easily have gone to Bethany, or Caesarea, or Capernaum, all of which were more easily accessible to Jerusalem than Rome. The Catholic view is highly speculative.

Peter Was Not the First Pope

✓ No apostle attained supremacy in New Testament times.

✓ No New Testament epistle teaches that Peter became pope.

✓ Paul affirmed he was not inferior to *any* other apostle (including Peter).

✓ The history of the early church in the book of Acts argues against the existence of a papacy.

✓ Peter was not infallible.

✓ Peter's name being listed first shows only his importance—not his papacy.

✓ The "rock" upon which the church would be built was not Peter but his *confession of faith* that Jesus is the Christ (Matthew 16:18).

✓ The "keys of the kingdom" relate only to Peter's privilege of preaching the gospel.

✓ Jesus' prayer that Peter's faith would not fail relates only to his restoration following his denial of Christ (Luke 22:31,32).

✓ Jesus' instruction to "tend My sheep" was given not to elevate Peter over the other apostles but to bring him back up to their level.

✓ The claim that Peter ended up in Rome is problematic.

 For further information on the Catholic view of Peter as the first pope, consult *Reasoning from the Scriptures with Catholics*, pages 85–120.

The Pope, the Bishops, and the Magisterium

Are Fallible

Power in the Roman Catholic Church centers in the pope—"the Supreme Pontiff." He is said to be the "Vicar of Christ" on earth. (Vicar literally means "one serving as a substitute or agent.") The pope as "Vicar of Christ" acts for and in the place of Christ. As successor to Peter, the pope exercises authority over the 3250 bishops in the Church.[1]

The bishops themselves are viewed as the successors of Christ's apostles. According to the Second Vatican Council, the bishops "have by divine institution taken the place of the apostles as pastors of the Church, in such wise that whoever listens to them is listening to Christ and whoever despises them despises Christ and him who sent Christ."[2]

Catholics believe there is biblical support for their view that the bishops are the successors of the apostles. They argue from Matthew 16:18 that Christ's words about the gates of Hades not overpowering the church point to the necessity of having a continuing line of authority on earth via "apostolic succession" (the bishops).[3] They also argue from Matthew 28:20 that Christ's "Great Commission" involved a promise to be with the apostles to the end of the age, which would require that there be successors to the apostles who would be present until the end of the age.[4] Further, Catholics infer from John 20:23 that Christ transferred the power to forgive sins to the apostles and their successors.

Infallibility

Many distinctive Catholic doctrines have come from the allegedly infallible teachings of the popes. Catholics believe that when the pope speaks *ex cathedra* (Latin, meaning "from the chair") on issues pertaining to faith and morals, he is infallible. Indeed, we are told, the Spirit of truth (the Holy Spirit) guarantees that, when the pope declares he is teaching infallibly as Christ's representative and visible head of the Church on matters of faith and practice, he cannot lead the church into error.[5] When speaking on matters of faith and morals, the pope can neither deceive *nor be deceived.* When not speaking *ex cathedra,* however, it is possible that the pope could be fallible in something he says or teaches.

Papal Infallibility

The Roman Pontiff "enjoys this infallibility in virtue of his office, when, as supreme pastor and teacher of all the faithful...he proclaims in an absolute decision a doctrine pertaining to faith or morals" (Second Vatican Council).

Not only is the pope infallible when speaking *ex cathedra* on matters of faith and practice, the bishops too are infallible when they speak "with one voice"—that is, when all the bishops agree on a doctrine. They are assured freedom from error "provided they are in union with the Bishop of Rome and their teaching is subject to his authority."[6]

Such a view is understandable in light of the Catholic teaching on *apostolic succession.* This refers to "the uninterrupted handing on" of episcopal power and authority from the apostles to contemporary bishops.[7] This transfer of episcopal power is effected whenever a validly ordained Catholic bishop ordains a successor by the laying on of hands. We are told that "those ordained as bishops have continued to fulfill the roles of the apostles, and have been continually in communion with the Apostolic See, that is, with the Bishop of Rome."[8]

The Teaching Magisterium

The teaching Magisterium is an outgrowth of the idea that the bishops are "infallible" when they speak with one voice on faith and morals. The *Magisterium* (from the Latin word for "master") is a body made up of the bishops and the pope. It functions as the authoritative teaching body of the church that safeguards doctrines. The purpose of this body is to ensure that the faithful do not go astray doctrinally. It alone has the right to interpret and judge the correct meaning of God's Word. It is believed that God protects this body from teaching falsehood in any way.

Sometimes Catholics argue in favor of the Magisterium by saying that it is the only means of preserving true unity in the church. Without the Magisterium, there would be doctrinal chaos. Without the Magisterium, denominations would emerge, each seeking to interpret the Bible as it saw fit.

The Pope, Bishops, and Magisterium: The Roman Catholic View

- The pope is the Vicar of Christ on earth.
- The bishops are the successors of Christ's apostles.
- The pope is infallible when he speaks *ex cathedra*.
- The bishops are infallible when they speak "with one voice" in agreement with the pope.
- The Magisterium is the authoritative teaching body of the church.

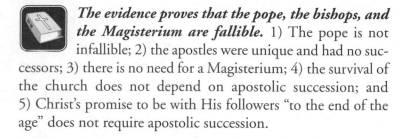

The evidence proves that the pope, the bishops, and the Magisterium are fallible. 1) The pope is not infallible; 2) the apostles were unique and had no successors; 3) there is no need for a Magisterium; 4) the survival of the church does not depend on apostolic succession; and 5) Christ's promise to be with His followers "to the end of the age" does not require apostolic succession.

The pope is not infallible. In claiming to be infallible when speaking on matters of faith and morals, the pope claims for himself something that even the apostles did not. The apostle Paul is an example. In the book of Galatians, Paul warned against the danger of a false gospel and proclaimed, "Even if we, or an angel from heaven, should preach to you a gospel contrary to what we have preached to you, he is to be accursed!" (Galatians 1:8). The gospel Paul preached is permanently recorded in written form in his epistles. And if anything conflicts with that written Scripture (even if it came *from him*), it is to be rejected. Scripture alone is infallible and hence authoritative (John 10:35).

When in Acts 17:11 the Bereans tested Paul's truth-claims against the Old Testament Scriptures, Paul did not chasten them but rather commended them. Communicate to your Catholic friend that we should follow the policy of the Bereans in regard to the truth-claims of the pope. His teachings should be measured against the teachings of Scripture. When this is done, it becomes clear—at least in many cases—that the pope's teaching is unbiblical.

As a way of illustrating the fallibility of the pope, consider the Galileo debacle. Galileo was a scientist who was also a believing Christian, and he had a high regard for Scripture. When he, using one of the first telescopes, posited the theory that the sun, not the earth, was the center of the solar system, this rocked the boat with the pope and the Roman Catholic Church, which at that time held to the theological position of an earth-centered solar system. Galileo was promptly summoned by an Inquisition in 1632, was tried, and was pronounced "vehemently suspected of heresy."[9] From that point forward, he was forced to repeat the seven penitential psalms once a week for three years and was held under house arrest until his death in 1642.[10] This episode clearly undermines the Roman Catholic view of the infallibility of the pope.

 Catholics sometimes respond to this incident by suggesting that the pope was not speaking *ex cathedra* on this occasion.[11] The truth is that the pope was, and is, a finite human being, prone to mistakes as all other human beings are. Only God has infinite understanding and makes no mistakes. That is why His Word is infallible (John 10:35)—*it comes straight from Him* (2 Timothy 3:16). Scripture never promised there would be successors to Peter who would be divinely protected from error when speaking *ex cathedra*. This is a man-made doctrine.

 Alert your Catholic friend to the sad reality of "antipopes" in Roman Catholic history. There have been times in history when there has been more than one pope. In fact, scholars tell us there have been some 35 antipopes in the history of the Church.[12] When there are two popes at once, the Catholic is left in a dilemma: Which pope is the Vicar of Christ on earth? Which one is the phony? Which one makes infallible statements on morals and faith when he speaks *ex cathedra?*[13] Though many Catholics ignore this issue, it is a question that has never been satisfactorily answered.

The apostles were unique and had no successors. The uniqueness of the apostles is seen in the unique miraculous powers they possessed. The apostles were handpicked by God and were given special unmistakable "signs of an apostle" (2 Corinthians 12:12). These sign gifts included the ability to raise people from the dead on command (Matthew 10:8), heal incurable diseases (Matthew 10:8; John 9:1-7), and perform immediate exorcisms (Acts 16:16-18). On one occasion an apostle pronounced a supernatural death sentence on two people who had "lied to the Holy Spirit," and they immediately fell down dead (Acts 5:1-11).

Although the apostles and their miraculous confirmations have passed away, their teachings remain in authority through the pages of holy Scripture. "The authority of apostolic *writings* has replaced the authority of the first-century apostolic *writers.*"[14]

Related to this, we read in Jude 3: "Contend earnestly for the faith which was once for all handed down to the saints." In the Greek text, the definite article "the" preceding "faith" points to the one and only faith; there is no other. "The faith" refers to the apostolic body of truth that became regulative upon the church (see Acts 6:7; Galatians 1:23; 1 Timothy 4:1).[15] This "faith" or body of doctrine was *once for all handed down* to the saints by the *unique* apostles of God, and their message was confirmed by mighty miracles.

The word translated "once for all" (Greek, *apax*) refers to something that has been done for all time, something that never needs repeating. The revelatory process was finished after this "faith" had "once for all" been delivered by the apostles. Note also that the form of the verb "handed down" (an aorist passive participle) indicates an act completed in the past with no continuing element.

Scripture indicates that the church is built on the foundation of the prophets and apostles (Ephesians 2:20). Once a foundation is built, no further foundation is needed. And therefore there is no need for apostolic successors. Help your Catholic friend understand that *apostles* and *prophets* were foundational gifts to the church, and there is not a shred of biblical proof that there were to be successors to the apostles.

 We do not need a Magisterium. Contrary to the idea that we must submit our understanding of God's Word to an organization (the Magisterium), individual believers are exhorted and instructed by Scripture to test things for themselves (1 Thessalonians 5:21; 1 John 4:1). They are to be like the Bereans, who examined what the apostle Paul said in light of the Word of God to make sure that his teachings were in line with Scripture. (See Acts 17:11; also Galatians 1:8. Note that the Bereans were not priests; they were laypeople living in the city of Berea.)

Scripture alone is our spiritual guide, and the Holy Spirit alone is our teacher (see John 14:18,26). Each believer can study the Scriptures and come to a conviction, under the leading of the Holy Spirit, as to what the text means.

Protestants believe the Bible is clear *(perspicuous)*. As noted in Chapter 2, this is not to say that every verse and every doctrine in the Bible are equally clear, but that the main verses and the main doctrines *are* clear. As it's been said, in the Bible the main things are the plain things and the plain things are the main things.[16] An example of a "plain thing" that is a "main thing" is the fact that salvation comes by faith in Christ. Close to 200 references in the New Testament make this *main, plain* point (John 3:16 among them).

A big problem for the Catholic view is that even the teachings of the Magisterium need interpreting. For example, there are statements by the Magisterium on important issues like the role of Mary, tradition, and justification that have been interpreted *differently* through the years by various Roman Catholics. How, then, can the allegedly definitive interpretations of the Magisterium be authoritative, in view of the fact that they are subject to varying interpretations?

CAUTION Catholics often argue that the Magisterium is needed to ensure unity in the church, and they claim that the Roman Catholic Church is indeed a united church. The reality is that the Roman Catholic Church has been characterized by significant *dis*unity in recent years. One of the reasons the church published the new *Catechism of the Catholic Church* was to draw the church back to doctrinal unity. Debated issues include such critically important doctrines as the Trinity, the Eucharist, and the authority of the pope.[17]

The freedom to interpret the Scriptures is clearly a biblical doctrine (Acts 17:11). But it is important not to misunderstand what is being said here. Protestants who believe in this freedom also believe that God the Holy Spirit has given the church pastors and teachers, and that we should all learn from them. We can also learn from writings of the past (for example, those of the church fathers). We do not advocate a doctrinal free-for-all.

Scripture says we are to handle the Word of God rightly (2 Corinthians 4:2; 2 Peter 3:16). But it is *we* who do the handling—not the Roman Catholic Magisterium. And when we listen to a teacher or a pastor, or read something written by a church father, it is *we* who test those truth-claims against the infallible Word of God (1 Thessalonians 5:21; Acts 17:11).

The survival of the church does not depend on apostolic succession. Jesus said, "On this rock I will build My church, and the gates of Hades will not overpower it" (Matthew 16:18). Catholics are reading something into this verse that simply is not there. The fact is, the "gates of Hades" do not overpower the church because of the divine power of Jesus Christ, not because of any alleged apostolic succession.

 Emphasize to your Catholic friend that the church is *owned* by Jesus, since He purchased it with His own blood (Acts 20:28)—*and what He owns, He protects.* Christ is also called the *head* of the church (Ephesians 5:23), and since He is its head, it is *His* prerogative to protect it—not the prerogative of finite humans.

There are many expositors who apply this verse to the impending death of Christ, and there is some warrant for this interpretation. The Jews of New Testament times would have understood the "gates of Hades" to refer to *physical death.* Bible scholar Craig Keener notes that the "gates of Hades" in the Old Testament (Job 38:17; Psalm 9:13) and subsequent Jewish tradition referred to the realm and power of death.[18] This being so, Jesus may have been declaring to the disciples that His impending death on the cross would not prevent or stand in the way of His work of building the church.[19] Contextually, just a few verses later (Matthew 16:21), Jesus spoke of His death. It may be, then, that He was anticipating His death and His *victory over* death through the resurrection, after which He would become the head of the church and build it through the ages (Ephesians 5:23; Matthew 16:18).

Another possible interpretation, held by some evangelicals, is that death *in any form* will not silence the church—the death of Jesus, the death of the apostles, or the death of Christians anywhere. By Christ's divine power, the church will be sustained forever. But so-called apostolic successors are nowhere in view in this verse.

 Christ's promise to be with His followers "to the end of the age" does not require apostolic succession. Jesus said, "Go…and make disciples of all the nations,…

and lo, I am with you always, even to the end of the age"
(Matthew 28:19,20). This verse does not allude even remotely
to apostolic succession. Here, Jesus is simply promising His followers that He would be with them always. Keep in mind the
context—making disciples. As the disciples themselves made
other disciples, the new disciples would then go forward and
make more disciples, and then those disciples would go forward
and make even more disciples, *and so on*. As this process continued until the end of the age, Christ promised that He would
be with them.

The Pope, the Bishops, and the Magisterium Are Fallible

✓ The pope is not infallible.

✓ The apostles were unique and had no successors.

✓ There is no need for a Magisterium.

✓ The survival of the church does not depend on
apostolic succession.

✓ Christ's promise to be with His followers "to the
end of the age" does not require apostolic succession.

For further information on the Catholic view of the
pope, the bishops, and the Magisterium, consult *Reasoning from the Scriptures with Catholics*, pages 85–120.

5

Mary Was the Mother of Jesus,

Nothing More

 The Mary of Roman Catholicism is far different from the one portrayed in the pages of Scripture. In a number of ways, the Mary of Roman Catholicism is a powerful, almost godlike, being.

Mary is said to have been "immaculately conceived," and is viewed as beyond sin altogether—spotless, undefiled, holy, innocent in every way, pure in soul and body, stainless. All this was necessary in order for her to be an appropriate habitation for Christ. As well, Mary is said to have been *perpetually* a virgin—meaning she retained her virginal state both *during* the birth of Jesus and *afterward,* even though married to Joseph. Mary's womb, a "shrine" of the Holy Spirit, would have been defiled had she engaged in sexual relations with Joseph.[1]

Although there are New Testament references to Jesus' brothers (Matthew 13:55,56), these are really Jesus' cousins, we are told. It was common for Jews to refer to relatives as "brothers." Seen in this light, the fact that Jesus had "brothers" does not argue against Mary's perpetual virginity.

Mary is considered the "Mother of God" in Roman Catholic theology. This term is a "title of the blessed Virgin Mary as the physical parent of Jesus, who is God."[2] Jesus was true God, and Mary was truly the mother of Jesus.[3]

Many Catholics speak of Mary as the co-redeemer of humanity. After all, her agreement to bear in her womb the human–divine Messiah shows that she took part in the divine plan of redemption. Moreover, she is often portrayed as offering her son to the Father on Golgotha.

Catholics are careful to clarify what is meant when Mary is called "co-redeemer." The prefix "co" does not mean "equal," but means "with." Mary is not on an equal level with Jesus. Rather, she simply *shared* with her Son in the saving work of redemption.[4]

Mary is also called "Mediatrix of Grace." While Jesus is Mediator between man and God, Mary nevertheless holds a secondary mediatorship subordinate to Christ. Though grace comes *from* Christ, it is said to come *through* Mary. Jesus is the *Head* from which grace flows, but Mary is the *neck* through which it flows.[5]

Catholics believe that when Mary's life was over, she was bodily assumed into heaven. Because she was full of grace (Luke 1:28) and because she was preserved from original sin, she was allegedly kept from the consequences of sin—namely, corruption of the body after death.[6]

In view of the above, it is not surprising that Mary is venerated by Catholics worldwide. Catholics say the veneration they give Mary *(hyperdulia)* is less than the adoration they give God *(latria)*, but is nevertheless higher than that rendered to angels and other saints *(dulia)*.[7]

Mary: The Roman Catholic View

• Mary was immaculately conceived, and was thereby preserved from original sin.

- Mary perpetually remained a virgin, never engaging in sexual relations with Joseph.
- Mary is the Mother of God.
- Mary is a co-redeemer and mediatrix.
- Mary was bodily assumed into heaven following her earthly life.
- Mary is venerated by Catholics worldwide.

The Bible portrays Mary as simply the mother of Jesus, nothing more. Scripture provides evidence that 1) Mary was a humble bondservant of God; 2) Mary was not immaculately conceived and had a sin nature; 3) Mary was not a perpetual virgin; 4) Mary was the "mother of God" only in a narrowly defined sense; 5) Mary is not a co-redeemer or mediatrix; 6) Mary was not bodily assumed into heaven; and 7) Mary should not be venerated.

Mary was a humble bondservant of God. In many ways the Roman Catholic Mary ends up being a female counterpart to Jesus. Jesus was born without sin—Mary was conceived without original sin; Jesus was sinless—Mary lived a sinless life; Jesus ascended to heaven following His resurrection—Mary was bodily assumed into heaven at the end of her earthly life; Jesus is a Mediator—Mary is a mediatrix; Jesus is a Redeemer—Mary is a co-redeemer; Jesus is the King—Mary is the Queen of Heaven.[8] Yet *none* of these ideas are found anywhere within the pages of Scripture.

The Mary of the Bible is far different from the portrayal above. The biblical Mary is a "bondslave of the Lord" (Luke 1:38)—a humble servant of God. The Greek word for bondslave *(doulos)* speaks of one whose will is "swallowed up in the will of another," "one who serves another to the disregard of

[her] own interests."[9] Mary was not one who sought great devotion from others. The humble attitude of the biblical Mary is far removed from the tone of the veneration paid to her in Roman Catholicism.

 In view of the tremendous attention paid to Mary in Catholic churches, it might be instructive to ask Catholic friends to read through the New Testament over a few months and keep track of how much attention is given to Mary *(almost none)*. They may be very surprised.

The Bible indicates that Mary was a godly woman and was well-versed in the Old Testament Scriptures (see Luke 1:46-55). But she certainly was not gifted with any kind of supernatural insight into God's doings, as evidenced in Jesus' response to her when she and Joseph found Him in the temple as a child (Luke 2:39-50).[10]

Luke 1:48 indicates Mary is "blessed" among women. The question is, is this blessedness based on something *intrinsic* to Mary's own being that separates her from all other women and makes her *worthy* of such blessedness? Or is it simply based on the fact that God chose her to give birth to the Messiah? The context of Scripture indicates the latter is the case. Protestant apologists Elliot Miller and Ken Samples make this observation about the Mary of the Bible:

> Without wishing to detract from her rightful honor, it must be stated that Mary's part in the incarnation was merely as the vehicle chosen by the Triune God for the Logos's [Jesus'] entry into this world. After this she was also called to provide maternal care for the divine child. In Scripture, after these functions are accomplished she recedes into the background and we read little of her. (In this sense she has rightly been compared with John the Baptist, who, after he accomplished his preparatory

purpose, said: "He must increase while I must decrease" [John 2:30].)[11]

Jesus never exalted His mother Mary as Catholics have done. He is often seen downplaying His relationship with her. This is illustrated in the several occasions where He calls her "woman" instead of "mother" (John 2:1-4; 19:26), something that was not customary for a Jewish son to do.[12]

Mary was not immaculately conceived and had a sin nature. Biblically, it is clear that Mary was in the same spiritual condition as all other human beings. That is not to say Mary was a "bad person," or that she was as bad a sinner as every other sinner. But she definitely had a sin nature and was in need of a Savior. She knew this to be true of herself (Luke 1:47).

Every single human being—with the one exception of Jesus, whose conception was by the Holy Spirit (Luke 1:35)—has been born into the world with a sin nature. Romans 5:12 tells us that "through one man sin entered into the world, and death through sin, and so death spread to *all* men, because *all* sinned" (emphasis added). We are assured that "*all* have sinned and fall short of the glory of God" (Romans 3:23, emphasis added). "There is *none* righteous, *not even one*" (Romans 3:10, emphasis added). Jesus Himself asserted, "*No one* is good except God alone" (Luke 18:19, emphasis added).

Scripture indicates that Mary was in need of redemption as are all other people (Luke 1:47). In fact, she even presented an offering to the Jewish priest arising out of her state of sin (2:22-24).

Luke 1:28

Catholics cite Luke 1:28—"Hail, full of grace" (Catholic New American Bible)—in favor of Mary's alleged immaculate conception. They say this "grace" extends over her whole life, beginning with her entry into the world. However, the Greek is more accurately translated "favored one." This verse simply points to the favor granted to Mary in that she was chosen to bear the Messiah.

Mary was not a perpetual virgin. In Matthew 1:25 we read that Joseph "kept [Mary] a virgin *until* she gave birth to a Son; and he called His name Jesus" (emphasis added). The word "until" implies that normal sexual relations between Joseph and Mary took place following the birth of Jesus.

Luke 1:34

In Luke 1:34 Mary responded to Gabriel's words about Jesus being born in her womb by saying, "How can this be, since I am a virgin?" Catholics say that this indicates Mary had taken a lifelong vow of virginity. However, Matthew 1:18 says simply that Mary was engaged to Joseph at this time. After she got married, she had normal marital relations with Joseph (Matthew 1:24,25). She took no vow of virginity.

Further, when Jesus spoke in His hometown, some of the people there inquired: "Is not this the carpenter's son? Is not His mother called Mary, and His brothers, James and Joseph and Simon and Judas? And His sisters, are they not all with us?" (Matthew 13:55,56).

The Catholic claim that references to Jesus' "brothers" actually refer to cousins is not convincing. It is true that the Greek term for brother *(adelphos)* can be used in a sense not referring to a literal brother (for example, it can refer to *Jewish* brothers). Yet, unless the context indicates otherwise, Greek scholars agree the term should be taken in its normal sense of a literal brother. There was a perfectly appropriate word in the Greek language that could have been used in the biblical text for "cousin" *(anepsios)*, but this word is not used in the verses that speak of Jesus' brothers. Since these "brothers" are always mentioned as being *with* Mary, from the context it's clear that *literal* brothers are in view.

 In an Old Testament messianic prophecy that was literally fulfilled in the life of Jesus, we read: "I have become estranged from my brothers, and an alien to my mother's sons" (Psalm 69:8). That this psalm is messianic in nature[13] is clear by comparing verse 8 with John 7:3-5; verse 9 with John 2:17 and Romans 15:3; verse 21 with Matthew 27:34; and verse 25 with Matthew 23:38. Since verse 8 is a messianic reference to Christ's alienation from "my mother's sons," it's clear that Mary had other children besides Jesus.

Contrary to the Catholic view that sexual relations between Mary and Joseph would have defiled Mary, the biblical view is that sexual relations within marriage bring no defilement, but are good and proper (see Genesis 2:24; Matthew 19:5; Ephesians 5:31). Only sexual relations outside of marriage are condemned in Scripture (1 Corinthians 6:15,16).

 Mary was the "mother of God" only in a narrowly defined sense. Mary was first recognized as the "mother of God" at the Council of Ephesus in A.D. 431. That council carefully qualified the expression by declaring that Mary was the "mother of God according to the manhood" of Jesus. Mary was truly the mother of Christ's human nature and was the "mother of God" in the limited sense that she conceived and bore the Second Person of the Trinity, not according to His divine nature, but only according to His assumed human nature.

In view of the fact that Mary did not give rise to the divinity of Jesus but was only the human instrument through whom the incarnation took place, *there is nothing in this doctrine that exalts Mary at all.* Mary is not the mother of Christ's deity. Although the child born in her womb was divine, it was not *she* who gave rise to that divinity. Her role was to enable Jesus as eternal God to take on an additional nature—a human nature. We need to make sure our Roman Catholic friends understand this distinction.

Mary is not a co-redeemer or mediatrix. Scripture is clear there is only one mediator between man and God, and that is Jesus. No secondary mediator or mediatrix is needed: "There is one God, and one mediator also between God and men, the man Christ Jesus" (1 Timothy 2:5). When this one mediator died on the cross, it was not Mary who offered Him to the Father (as Catholics claim), but rather Christ, who "offered Himself without blemish to God" (Hebrews 9:14).

It is noteworthy that Scripture says that *only God* can be Savior. God Himself (Yahweh) said in Isaiah 43:11: "I, even I, am the LORD; and there is no Savior besides Me." The fact that Jesus is portrayed as Savior in the New Testament shows His unique divinity (Titus 2:13,14). It is through this one Savior and Him alone that "we have redemption, the forgiveness of sins" (Colossians 1:14).

The biblical doctrine of the Redeemer is closely tied to the doctrine of the incarnation. If Christ the Redeemer had been only God, He could not have died, since God by His very nature cannot die. It was only as a man that Christ could represent humanity and die as a man. As God, however, Christ's death had infinite value, value sufficient to provide redemption for the sins of all humankind. Clearly, then, Christ had to be both God and man to secure man's salvation (1 Timothy 2:5).

Further, Scripture reveals that the Redeemer must of necessity be sinless. Hebrews 4:15 tells us, "We do not have a high priest who cannot sympathize with our weaknesses, but One who has been tempted in all things as we are, yet without sin" (see also 2 Corinthians 5:21). Just as lambs with no defects were used in Old Testament sacrifices, so the Redeemer was the spotless Lamb of God who was unblemished by sin (1 Peter 1:19).

 Jesus' unique qualification as Redeemer is precisely what *dis*qualifies Mary from any role as a co-redeemer, because Mary 1) is a mere human (she is not divine), who 2) is defiled by sin (Romans 3:10-12,23; 5:12) and who 3) is herself in need of a Redeemer (Luke 1:47). Help your Catholic friend understand this.

Whereas one will look in vain for Scripture references that portray Mary as a co-redeemer, one will find numerous references to the effect that Jesus exclusively is man's means of coming into a relationship with God. Jesus Himself said, "I am the way, and the truth, and the life; no one comes to the Father but through Me" (John 14:6). As Peter boldly proclaimed, "There is salvation in no one else; for there is no other name under heaven that has been given among men by which we must be saved" (Acts 4:12).

 Many Catholics will respond that Jesus is the *primary* Mediator, and that Mary's role is only *secondary*. The point to emphasize is that *Mary has no role whatsoever* other than being the divinely chosen human instrument through whom the divine Redeemer would be born into the world. That being accomplished, the biblical record assigns no further role to Mary.

Mary was not bodily assumed into heaven. Even Catholic theologians admit there is no direct scriptural proof for this doctrine.[14] In view of this—*and* in view of the fact that this doctrine did not even become dogma for the Roman Catholic Church until the middle of the twentieth century—we can assume it is not true, but rather is a manmade doctrine. The reality is, the time and circumstances of Mary's death are completely unknown. We can say, though, that the *fact* of her death was something that was generally accepted by the church fathers.[15]

Why did Mary die? She died for the same reason all other humans die. She, like us, was subject to the penalty of sin, which is death (see Genesis 2:17; Romans 6:23). This is precisely why she, like us, needed a Savior (Luke 1:47).

Mary should not be venerated. As we read the Gospels, we are given the teachings of Jesus—yet nowhere in His teachings do we find that Mary is to be exalted or venerated. As we read the epistles, written by the apostles for the spiritual instruction of the church, nowhere do we find anything about the exaltation or veneration of Mary. There is much in all these books about worship and salvation and prayer and many other very important doctrines, but *nothing about the exaltation or veneration of Mary.*

Luke 1:42

Catholics say that Elizabeth's words to Mary—"Blessed are you among women"—supports the veneration of Mary. However, "blessed" does not mean that she is to be venerated. Mary is blessed *among* women, not exalted *above* women. She is blessed because of her privilege of bearing the Lord in her womb.

We would naturally think that if Mary plays the important roles attributed to her by the Roman Catholic Church (co-redeemer, mediatrix, and the like), there would be at least something about all this in the pages of Scripture. Yet there is nothing. In the epistles Mary's name is virtually absent—and these books are precisely where one would expect Mary's name to be most prominent if the Roman Catholic exaltation and veneration of her were correct. Any Catholic who looks at the evidence must admit that biblical support for Mary's veneration is lacking.

Mary Was the Mother of Jesus, Nothing More

✓ Mary was a humble bondservant of God.

✓ Mary was not immaculately conceived and had a sin nature.

✓ Mary was not a perpetual virgin.

✓ Mary was the "mother of God" only in a narrowly defined sense.

✓ Mary is not a co-redeemer or mediatrix.

✓ Mary was not bodily assumed into heaven.

✓ Mary should not be venerated.

For further information on the Catholic view of Mary, consult *Reasoning from the Scriptures with Catholics*, pages 257–322.

6

Justification Is Instantaneous,

Once-for-All, and Entirely by Grace

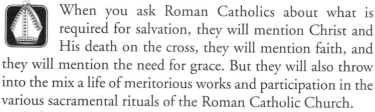 When you ask Roman Catholics about what is required for salvation, they will mention Christ and His death on the cross, they will mention faith, and they will mention the need for grace. But they will also throw into the mix a life of meritorious works and participation in the various sacramental rituals of the Roman Catholic Church.

Catholics believe that the salvation process starts out with "first actual grace." This grace is "first" in the sense that it is God who initially reaches out to a person and gives him the grace that will enable him to seek God, have faith, and prepare his soul for baptism and justification. It is "actual" in the sense that good acts are the goal.

This grace does not have an automatic influence. A person must respond to it—*yield to its influence*—for it to become effectual. Should a person cooperate with this grace, he or she will end up performing "salutary acts" that prepare the soul for baptism and justification. If he rejects this grace and ends up dying, he is lost.

When a person is finally baptized, original sin is said to be removed from the soul and in its place sanctifying grace is "infused." At this point the person experiences "initial justification." No one can merit or earn this grace, and hence this initial aspect of justification is said to be by grace. When the soul is infused with this sanctifying grace of God, inherent righteousness becomes one of the soul's characteristics.

The backdrop to all this is that when Adam and Eve fell into sin, they lost the divine life God had bestowed upon them through sanctifying grace. Since then, every human being born into the world has been born without this divine life or sanctifying grace. For a person to be saved, there must be a *restoration* of sanctifying grace. At the moment of baptism, this is exactly what happens. As a result of this infusion of sanctifying grace, the person experiences "initial justification."

Catholics believe that following initial justification, there is a second aspect of justification that occurs throughout life as the person continues to cooperate with God's grace and progresses in good works, thereby meriting the further grace that is necessary for him or her to enter eternal life. This means the person must *sustain* his new relationship with God and *continue* cooperating with God's grace to gain full and final justification. He must be cautious along the way not to commit a mortal sin (a conscious, deliberate, serious sin), which has the effect of erasing grace from the soul. The believer will only know for certain that he or she is finally justified at the end of the process (that is, when he or she dies).

Taken in its totality, Roman Catholicism espouses a works system of salvation. According to Catholics, salvation does involve grace and faith, but it is not by *grace alone* through *faith alone,* as the Reformers taught. Grace alone is not sufficient, without human works, to yield final and full justification. While Catholics acknowledge the *necessity* of grace, they do not acknowledge the *exclusivity* of grace.

"Justification by Grace"

When you hear a Roman Catholic say, "We believe in justification by grace," he is referring only to the first aspect of justification—"initial justification." Though this justification begins by God's grace, it is back-loaded with lots of things one must do.

One of the more disturbing aspects of Roman Catholic theology is the teaching that the grace of justification can be gained and lost and gained and lost, on and on. It is a *conditional* justification. Catholics believe that committing a mortal sin virtually erases sanctifying and justifying grace from the soul. For a person who commits such a sin, the only remedy is to become "re-justified" through the sacrament of penance. (More on this later in chapter 8.)

Justification: The Roman Catholic View

- Since Adam and Eve, humans are born into the world devoid of "sanctifying grace."

- For a person to be saved, sanctifying grace must be restored to the soul.

- Toward this end, the process of salvation starts out with "first actual grace."

- As one cooperates with first actual grace, one performs "salutary acts," which prepare the soul for baptism and justification.

- At baptism, original sin is removed, sanctifying grace is infused into the soul, and one experiences "initial justification."

- The second aspect of justification occurs *throughout life* as one continues to cooperate with God's grace and progresses in good works.

The Bible teaches that justification is a once-for-all event based entirely on God's grace and received through faith alone. Scripture teaches that 1) justification is a singular and instantaneous event; 2) justification involves a legal declaration by God; 3) justification is external to man; 4) justification is once-for-all; 5) justification is based on the work of Christ on the cross; 6) the result of justification is peace with God; 7) justification comes through faith alone; 8) justification is based entirely on God's grace; and 9) good works are a *consequence of* justification, not a *condition for* it.

Justification is a singular and instantaneous event. The Bible portrays justification as a singular event in which God declares the believing sinner to be righteous. It is not based on performance or good works. It involves God's instantaneous pardoning of the sinner, declaring him or her to be absolutely righteous at the moment he or she trusts in Christ for salvation (see Romans 3:25,28,30; 8:33,34; Galatians 4:21–5:12; 1 John 1:7–2:2).

Justification involves a legal declaration by God. Negatively, this word means that a person is once-for-all pronounced *not guilty* before God. Positively, the word means that a person is once-for-all pronounced *righteous* before God. The very righteousness of Christ is imputed (or credited) to the believer's life. From the moment a person places faith in Christ the Savior, God sees that person through the lens of Christ's righteousness.

This view is often referred to as "forensic justification." "Forensic" comes from a Latin word meaning "forum." This word has its roots in the fact that in the ancient Roman forum, a court could meet and make judicial, or legal, declarations. Forensic justification, then, speaks of God's judicial declaration of the believer's righteousness before Him. The believer is legally acquitted of all guilt, and the very righteousness of Christ is imputed to his account. Henceforth, when God sees the believer, He sees him in all the righteousness of Christ.

Justification is external to man, and it does not hinge on man's *personal* level of righteousness. It does not hinge on anything that man does. It hinges solely on God's declaration. Even while the person is still a sinner and is experientially not righteous, he is nevertheless righteous *in God's sight* because of forensic justification.

This view of justification has support from the Old Testament. For example, in Deuteronomy 25:1 we read of judges who "*justify the righteous* and condemn the wicked" (emphasis added). The word *justify* here clearly means "declare to be righteous" just as *condemn* means "declare to be guilty." The word is used in a forensic sense here and elsewhere in the Old Testament (see, for example, Job 27:5 and Proverbs 17:15). When the apostle Paul (an Old Testament scholar par excellence) used the word *justify* in the Book of Romans, he did so against this Old Testament backdrop.[1]

Justification is once-for-all. At the moment a person places personal faith in Christ, God makes an incalculable "deposit" of righteousness into that person's personal "spiritual bank account." It is a *once-for-all* act on God's part. It is *irrevocable*. It is a "done deal." It cannot be lost. God's pronouncement is final. This is the wonderful gift of salvation.

Justification is based on the work of Christ on the cross. God did not just subjectively decide to overlook man's sin or wink at his unrighteousness. Justification has an objective basis. Indeed, Jesus died on the cross for us. He died in our stead and paid for our sins. Jesus ransomed us from death by His own death on the cross (2 Corinthians 5:21).

There has been a great exchange. As the great reformer Martin Luther put it, "Lord Jesus, you are my righteousness, I am your sin. You have taken upon yourself what is mine and given me what is yours. You have become what You were not so that I might become what I was not."[2]

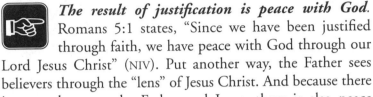

The result of justification is peace with God. Romans 5:1 states, "Since we have been justified through faith, we have peace with God through our Lord Jesus Christ" (NIV). Put another way, the Father sees believers through the "lens" of Jesus Christ. And because there is peace between the Father and Jesus, there is also peace between the Father and believers, since believers are "in Christ" (Romans 8:1).

If a person were to look through a piece of red glass, everything would appear red. If a person were to look through a piece of blue glass, everything would appear blue. If a person were to look through a piece of yellow glass, everything would appear yellow, and so on. Likewise, when we believe in Jesus Christ as our Savior, God looks at us *through the Lord Jesus Christ.* He sees us in all the pure white holiness of His Son. Help your Catholic friend understand this.

Justification comes through faith alone. Scripture clearly teaches justification by faith in Christ alone (Romans 4:1-25; Galatians 3:6-14). God justifies "the one who has faith in Jesus" (Romans 3:26). "A man is justified by faith apart from works of the Law" (Romans 3:28). "Abraham believed God, and it was credited to him as righteousness" (Romans 4:3). "Since we have been justified through faith, we have peace with God through our Lord Jesus Christ" (Romans 5:1 NIV).

Justification is based entirely on God's grace. Romans 3:24 tells us that God's declaration of righteousness is given to believers "freely by his grace" (NIV). The word *grace* literally means "unmerited favor." It is because of God's unmerited favor that believers can freely be "declared righteous" before God.

The Bible makes virtually no reference to "sanctifying grace." In the Bible, grace is quite simply *grace*—and it refers to the unmerited favor of God. "Unmerited" means it cannot be worked for. But Catholicism teaches that one must do meritorious works to *earn* grace. If grace is not free, though, it is not truly grace. "If it is by grace, it is no longer on the basis of works, otherwise grace is no longer grace" (Romans 11:6).

Further, the idea that God's grace is repeatedly communicated to His people through "sacraments" has no biblical basis. God's grace is given to us not through ritual ceremonies but comes straight from Him to all who believe in the person of Jesus Christ: "Having been justified by faith, we have peace with God through our Lord Jesus Christ, through whom also we have obtained our introduction by faith into this grace in which we stand; and we exult in hope of the glory of God" (Romans 5:1,2).

Contrary to Roman Catholicism, merit plays no role in obtaining eternal life. From a biblical perspective, opting for the merit system can only be bad, since all of us "merit" one thing—*eternal death*—"for the wages of sin is death, but the free gift of God is eternal life in Christ Jesus our Lord" (Romans 6:23).

We simply cannot do good works to earn favor with God. Rather, our favor with God comes only as a result of placing faith in Christ, after which time the Father sees us as being "in Christ." Experientially we may still be quite imperfect. But the Father sees us as having the very perfection of Christ since we are "in Christ" (Romans 8:1). As a result of our relationship with Christ, and as a result of walking in dependence on the Spirit, good works are increasingly produced in our lives. Good works are the *result* of our relationship with Christ, not the *source* of it.

One of my favorite passages in the Bible is Psalm 130:3,4: "If you, O LORD, kept a record of sins, O Lord, who could stand? But with you there is forgiveness" (NIV). This passage is brimming with grace. The phrase "kept a record" referred, among the ancients, to keeping an itemized account. The point of the psalmist is that if God were keeping a detailed account of all our sins, there would be no way for us to have a relationship with Him. It would be impossible. The good news is that God does not keep such an itemized account but rather forgives those who trust in Christ.

True grace is sometimes hard for people to grasp. After all, our society is performance-oriented. Obtaining good grades in school depends on how well we perform in school. Climbing up the corporate ladder at work depends on how well we perform at work. In our society, nothing of any real worth is a "free ticket." But God's gift of salvation is a grace-gift. *It is free!* We cannot attain it by a good performance. Ephesians 2:8,9 affirms this: "By grace you have been saved through faith; and that not of yourselves, it is the gift of God; not as a result of works, so that no one may boast." Titus 3:5 tells us that God "saved us, not on the basis of deeds which we have done in righteousness, but according to His mercy."

By contrast, Romans 3:20 says that "by the works of the Law no flesh will be justified [or declared righteous] in His sight" (insert added). In Galatians 2:16 the apostle Paul tells us that "a man is not justified by the works of the Law but through faith in Christ Jesus."

 Gifts cannot be worked for—only wages can be worked for. As Romans 4:4,5 tells us, "When a man works, his wages are not credited to him as a gift, but as an obligation. However, to the man who does not work but trusts God who justifies the wicked, his faith is credited as righteousness" (NIV). Since salvation is a free gift, *it cannot be earned.* Continually emphasize this point to your Catholic friend.

 ***Good works are a* consequence of *justification, not a* condition for *it.* Good works are a by-product of salvation (Matthew 7:15-23; 1 Timothy 5:10,25). Good works result from the changed purpose for living that salvation brings (1 Corinthians 3:10-15). We are not saved *by* our works, but in order *to do* good works. We do works not to *get* salvation, but because we have *already gotten* it.

 Catholics will often respond by arguing that James 2:17,26 teaches that good works are necessary for final salvation or justification. After all, in James 2:17 we read: "Faith, if it has no works, is dead, being by itself." Verse 26 likewise says, "Just as the body without the spirit is dead, so also faith without works is dead."[3]

However, James in this passage is basically answering the question, "How can we tell whether or not a person has true faith?" All that follows in chapter 2 answers this question.

James begins by asking, "What use is it, my brethren, if a man says he has faith but he has no works? Can that faith save him?" (2:14). Notice the oft-neglected little word "says" ("What use is it, my brethren, if a man *says* he has faith?"). Some people have genuine faith; others have an empty *profession* of faith that is not real. The first group of people who have genuine faith have works to back up the fact that their faith is genuine. Those who make an empty profession of faith show their lack of true faith by the absence of works. So, James answers his question by pointing out that you can tell whether a person has true faith by the test of works.

Martin Luther said it best: James 2 is not teaching that a person is saved by works or by personal merit. Rather a person is "justified" (declared righteous before God) by faith alone, but *not by a faith that is alone*. In other words, genuine faith will always result in or be accompanied by good works in the saved person's life.

Keep in mind that James was writing to Jewish Christians ("to the twelve tribes"—James 1:1) who were in danger of giving nothing but lip-service to Jesus. His intent, therefore, was to distinguish true faith from false faith. He shows that true faith results in works, which become visible evidences of faith's invisible presence. In other words, good works are the "vital signs" indicating that faith is alive.

Apparently some of these Jewish Christians had made a false claim of faith. It is this spurious boast of faith that James was condemning. Merely *claiming* to have faith is insufficient. Genuine faith is evidenced by works. Indeed,

> Workless faith is worthless faith; it is unproductive, sterile, barren, dead! Great claims may be made about a corpse that is supposed to have come to life, but if it does not move, if there are no vital signs, no heartbeat, no perceptible pulse, it is still dead. The false claims are silenced by the evidence.[4]

 Apart from the spirit, the body is dead; it is a lifeless corpse. By analogy, apart from the evidence of good works, faith is dead. It is lifeless and nonproductive. That is what James is teaching in James 2:17,26. His focus is on the *nature of faith,* not on the *reward of works.* After pointing this out, read aloud from Romans 3:20 and then ask, "Do you agree with what the apostle Paul says in this verse?"

Justification Is Instantaneous, Once-for-All, and Entirely by Grace

✓ Justification is a singular and instantaneous event.

✓ Justification involves a legal declaration by God.

✓ Justification is external to man.

✓ Justification is once-for-all.

✓ Justification is based on the work of Christ on the cross.

✓ The result of justification is peace with God.

✓ Justification comes through faith alone.

✓ Justification is based entirely on God's grace.

✓ Good works are a *consequence of* justification, not a *condition for* it.

For further information on the Catholic view of justification, consult *Reasoning from the Scriptures with Catholics,* pages 121–70.

The Sacrament of the Mass

Does Not Appease God

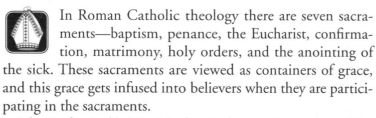 In Roman Catholic theology there are seven sacraments—baptism, penance, the Eucharist, confirmation, matrimony, holy orders, and the anointing of the sick. These sacraments are viewed as containers of grace, and this grace gets infused into believers when they are participating in the sacraments.

The Eucharist (or Mass) is the single most important of the Roman Catholic sacraments. It involves a resacrificing of Jesus (or, more accurately, a "re-presenting" or "renewing" of the sacrifice of Jesus) over and over again. Catholics say the Mass constitutes a "true and proper sacrifice,"[1] and in every single Mass *God is appeased.* The same Christ who offered himself in a *bloody* manner on the cross is, during the Mass (or Eucharist), present and offered in an *unbloody* manner.[2]

Catholics believe that during the Mass, the bread and wine miraculously turn into the actual body and blood of Christ. This happens at the prayer of consecration of the priest. Even though the bread and wine still *look* and *feel* and *taste* like bread and wine, they allegedly change into Jesus in His full deity and humanity.[3] The theological term used to describe this is "transubstantiation"—from the Latin term *transubstan-tiato*, meaning "change of substance." Catholics often cite the words of Jesus in John 6:51-55 in support of this doctrine. (I'll discuss this passage later in the chapter.)

Once the bread and wine are transformed into the body and blood of Jesus at the prayer of consecration, He is upon the altar as a sacrificial victim. He is then offered up as a living sacrifice. The priest prays: "We offer to you, God of glory and majesty, this holy and perfect sacrifice, the bread of life and the cup of eternal salvation."[4] This sacrifice is said to soothe God's wrath and cover people's sins. Catholics sometimes appeal to Hebrews 9:12 in support of this doctrine. (I'll discuss this verse later in the chapter.)

Catholics claim the sacrament of the Mass does not detract from the atonement Christ wrought on the cross, but is the primary means of applying the benefits of Christ's death to the faithful. The Mass is said to be "the source and summit of the Christian life."[5]

Attendance Required

Refusing to attend Mass is considered a mortal sin by Catholics. There are some legitimate reasons for missing it (like sickness). But *deliberately* choosing not to attend is a damning sin.

The Mass: The Roman Catholic View

- The Mass is the most important sacrament, involving a "re-presenting" of the sacrifice of Jesus.

- At the prayer of consecration, the bread and wine miraculously turn into the actual body and blood of Jesus. This is known as transubstantiation.

- Jesus is then upon the altar as a sacrificial victim. He is offered up as a living sacrifice.

- This sacrifice is said to soothe God's wrath and cover people's sins.

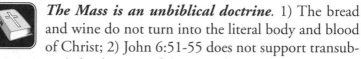 ***The Mass is an unbiblical doctrine.*** 1) The bread and wine do not turn into the literal body and blood of Christ; 2) John 6:51-55 does not support transubstantiation; 3) the doctrine of the Mass detracts from the atonement wrought by Christ; and 4) Hebrews 9:12 does not support the Mass.

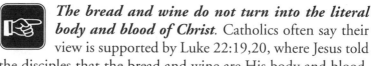 ***The bread and wine do not turn into the literal body and blood of Christ.*** Catholics often say their view is supported by Luke 22:19,20, where Jesus told the disciples that the bread and wine are His body and blood. But notice that Jesus was *physically present* with them when He said this. Obviously He intended His words to be taken figuratively.

Further, Scripture says drinking blood is forbidden to anyone (Genesis 9:4; Leviticus 3:17). The disciples, schooled in the commandments of God, would never have understood Jesus to be instructing them to go directly against these commandments.

Some months later, Peter even said, "I have never eaten anything unholy and unclean" (Acts 10:14). Peter could not have said this if he thought he had actually ingested the body and blood of Christ, for the law defines such an act as "unholy" and "unclean" (Leviticus 3:17). Further, the Jerusalem Council repeated an injunction contained in the Old Testament law to the effect that Christians are to abstain from blood (see Acts 15:29). This would not make much sense if those at the council thought they had actually drunk the real blood of Jesus.

Ask your Catholic friend, "In view of the scriptural teaching that drinking blood is forbidden, do you think the disciples, schooled in the commandments of God, would have understood Jesus to be instructing them to go directly against these commandments?"

Jesus often used figurative language. In fact, at the end of His upper-room discourse, He acknowledged this: "These things I have spoken to you *in figurative language"* (John 16:25, emphasis added). Jesus also often used figurative language when He taught by the use of parables (Matthew 13 and forward). His consistent use of figurative language certainly fits in with His instruction regarding the intended meaning of the Lord's Supper: "Do this *in remembrance* of Me" (Luke 22:19, emphasis added).

A major problem arises when we consider that Roman Catholic churches *all over the world* have Masses on a regular basis. This would require that Christ's human body be omnipresent (everywhere-present). As theologian Millard Erickson notes, "To believe that Jesus was in two places at once is something of a denial of the incarnation, which limited his physical human nature to one location."[6] The Scriptures clearly indicate that Christ's human body is *localized in heaven* (see Revelation 1:13-16). When Stephen was being stoned, he said, "Behold, I see the heavens opened up and the Son of Man standing at the right hand of God" (Acts 7:56). Scripturally speaking, only Christ's divine nature is omnipresent (Matthew 18:20; 28:20; John 1:47-49), not His human nature.

Ask your Catholic friend about some of the issues raised above. If Catholic churches all over the world hold Mass every Sunday, wouldn't Jesus' human body have to be everywhere-present? Doesn't Scripture teach that *only* Christ's divine nature—not His human nature (and body)—is everywhere-present? Doesn't

Scripture consistently portray Christ's human body as now being localized in heaven (Revelation 1:13-16)?

The memorial view of the Lord's Supper makes much more sense. In this view there is no change in the elements, and the ordinance is not intended to be a means of communicating grace to the participant. The bread and wine are purely symbols and reminders of Jesus in His death and resurrection (1 Corinthians 11:24,25). It also reminds us of the basic facts of the gospel (11:26), our anticipation of the second coming (11:26), and our oneness as the body of Christ (10:17). This viewpoint, I believe, best fits the context of 1 Corinthians 11:24-26.

 John 6:51-55 does not support transubstantiation. In this passage we read the following words of Jesus:

"I am the living bread that came down out of heaven; if anyone eats of this bread, he will live forever; and the bread also which I will give for the life of the world is My flesh."

Then the Jews began to argue with one another, saying, "How can this man give us His flesh to eat?"

So Jesus said to them, "Truly, truly, I say to you, unless you eat the flesh of the Son of Man and drink His blood, you have no life in yourselves. He who eats My flesh and drinks My blood has eternal life, and I will raise him up on the last day. For My flesh is true food, and My blood is true drink."

Catholics often cite this verse in support of transubstantiation. They argue that Jesus' listeners understood Him to be speaking literally, and hence transubstantiation must be the correct view.[7]

A look at the broader context helps us to see this is not the case. Contextually, Jesus had just performed a tremendous miracle by feeding 5000 people with five barley loaves and two fishes. Then, in verse 27, Jesus launched into His main message: "Do not work for the food which perishes, but for the food which endures to eternal life, which the Son of Man will give to you, for on Him the Father, God, has set His seal" (John 6:27). The crowd had eaten a meal that satisfied their *physical* hunger, but Christ wanted to give them something to satisfy their *spiritual* hunger—eternal life. It comes by partaking of the bread of life—Jesus—by faith.

The context for understanding Jesus' statement in John 6:54 ("He who eats My flesh and drinks My blood has eternal life") is set for us 15 verses earlier, in John 6:40: "This is the will of My Father, that everyone who beholds the Son and *believes in Him* will have eternal life; and I Myself will raise him up on the last day" (emphasis added). Contextually, the discussion centers on salvation by believing in Jesus, not on the Lord's Supper.

John 6:53,54 is therefore saying that just as one must consume or partake of physical food to sustain physical life, so one must spiritually appropriate Christ to have spiritual life. Just as the ancient Jews were dependent on manna (bread) to sustain physical life, so we are dependent on Jesus (the bread of life) for our spiritual life. Food that is eaten and then digested is assimilated so that it becomes a part of the body. Likewise, people must spiritually appropriate Christ and become one with Him *by faith* to receive the gift of eternal life.

The references to "flesh" and "blood" in this passage point us to the work of Christ on the cross. It was there that His flesh was nailed to the cross and His blood was shed to make man's salvation possible. By placing faith in the crucified Christ, we appropriate Him and His work of salvation.

 There is no mention of wine in John 6:48-58. If this passage were referring to the Mass, wouldn't wine be mentioned along with the bread? Be sure to ask your Catholic friend about this.

Catholics often respond that some of Jesus' listeners understood Him to be speaking *literally* when He announced that people were to eat of His flesh (John 6:52). However, the fact that some of Jesus' Jewish listeners understood Him this way does not prove that the Catholic position is correct, for indeed, the Jews often misunderstood what Jesus taught. When Jesus spoke of destroying "this temple," after which He would raise it again in three days, the Jews misunderstood and thought Jesus was referring to the literal temple made of stones (John 2:19-21; other misunderstandings are found in 3:4; 4:15; and 6:32-34). Just because some Jews may have understood Jesus to be referring to literal flesh in John 6 does not mean this interpretation is correct. The context indicates that Jesus was speaking figuratively of believing in Him for salvation (see verse 40).

The Bible often uses the language of eating and drinking to speak of our relationship with God.[8] We read, "O taste and see that the LORD is good; how blessed is the man who takes refuge in Him!" (Psalm 34:8). David, while in the wilderness of Judah, prayed, "My soul thirsts for You" (Psalm 63:1). He later affirmed, "My soul is satisfied as with marrow and fatness, and my mouth offers praises with joyful lips" (Psalm 63:5). The psalmist also said, "How sweet are Your words to my taste! Yes, sweeter than honey to my mouth" (Psalm 119:103). In 1 Peter 2:2,3 we read of longing "for the pure milk of the word, so that by it you may grow in respect to salvation, if you have tasted the kindness of the Lord." In Hebrews 5:14 we read, "Solid food is for the mature, who because of practice have their senses trained to discern good and evil." These are all simple metaphors pointing to spiritual realities. The same is true of John 6:51-55.

 The Mass detracts from the atonement wrought by Christ. The Catholic Council of Trent said: "This sacrifice [of the Mass] is truly propitiatory....For by this oblation the Lord is appeased…and he pardons wrongdoing and sins, even grave ones."[9] Because the Mass is said to bring about the forgiveness of sins, it is a necessity in the Catholic system of salvation. This *very much* detracts from the finality of the salvation Christ accomplished at the cross.

The idea that the Mass involves a repetition of the sacrifice of Christ is reminiscent of the repeated sacrifices of the old covenant, which were "a reminder of sins year by year" (Hebrews 10:3). Instead of believers having the full assurance of *complete* forgiveness of sins through the *once-for-all* sacrifice of Christ (Hebrews 10:12), the Mass gives a constant reminder of sins and remaining guilt to be atoned for week after week.[10]

Contrary to such repetition, there were three magnificent words in regard to His sacrificial death that Jesus uttered upon the cross: "It is finished" (John 19:30). This proclamation from the Savior's lips is fraught with meaning. The Lord was doing more than announcing the termination of His physical life. That fact was self-evident. What was not known by those who were carrying out the brutal business at Calvary was that somehow, despite the sin they were committing, *God through Christ had completed the final sacrifice for sin.* The work long contemplated, long promised, long expected by prophets and saints (Isaiah 53:4-6; Zechariah 12:10), is *done.*

The phrase "it is finished" can also be translated "paid in full." The backdrop to this is that in ancient days, whenever someone was found guilty of a crime, the offender was put in jail and a "certificate of debt" was posted on the jail door. This certificate listed all the crimes the offender was found guilty of. Upon release, after serving the prescribed time in jail, the offender was given the certificate of debt, and on it was stamped "paid in full." Christ took the certificate of debt of all our lives (including all our sins) and nailed it on the cross (Colossians 2:14). And Jesus said "paid in full!" upon the cross (John 19:30).

Jesus' words therefore do not constitute a moan of defeat or a sigh of resignation. Rather, His words were a triumphant recognition that He had now fully accomplished what He came into the world to do. The work of redemption was completed at the cross. Nothing further needed to be done. He had paid in full the price of our redemption (2 Corinthians 5:21). And "when He had made purification of sins, He sat down at the right hand of the Majesty on high" (Hebrews 1:3), where He remains to this day.

 How can Jesus' statement, "It is finished!" (John 19:30), be reconciled with the continual *re-presenting* of Christ's sacrifice in the Mass? Be sure to ask your Catholic friend about this.

Jesus completed the work of redemption at the cross with a single, *once-for-all* sacrifice. No more sacrifices (or "re-presentings") would occur. As we read in the book of Hebrews, God assures believers that "their sins and their lawless deeds I will remember no more" (10:17). And "where there is forgiveness of these things, there is no longer any offering for sin" (10:18). Christ made a sacrificial offering "once for all when He offered up Himself" (7:27). He did so "not through the blood of goats and calves, but through His own blood, He entered the holy place once for all, having obtained eternal redemption" (9:12). So, by the death of Christ "we have been sanctified through the offering of the body of Jesus Christ once for all" (10:10).

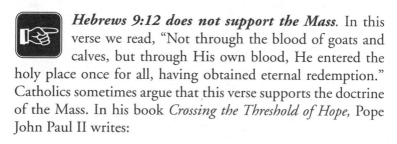 ***Hebrews 9:12 does not support the Mass.*** In this verse we read, "Not through the blood of goats and calves, but through His own blood, He entered the holy place once for all, having obtained eternal redemption." Catholics sometimes argue that this verse supports the doctrine of the Mass. In his book *Crossing the Threshold of Hope,* Pope John Paul II writes:

The Church is the instrument of man's salvation. It both contains and continually draws upon the mystery of Christ's redemptive sacrifice. Through the shedding of His own blood, Jesus Christ constantly "enters into God's sanctuary thus obtaining eternal redemption" (cf. Hebrews 9:12).[11]

Apologist James McCarthy has made some keen observations for us in regard to this quote from the pope's book[12]:

- The biblical text of Hebrews 9:12 reads, "Through His own blood, He entered the holy place once for all, having obtained eternal redemption." "Entered" is an aorist tense in the Greek, indicating a one-time past event. Yet the pope renders it in the present tense, "enters."

- Though the wording of Hebrews 9:12 is changed from what is recorded in Scripture, the pope puts it in quotation marks, implying that the source of His words is in fact Hebrews 9:12.

- The pope adds "constantly" ("constantly 'enters into God's sanctuary'") and leaves out "once for all."

- The pope changes the once-for-all "*having obtained* eternal redemption" so that it reads, "*thus obtaining* eternal redemption" (emphasis added).

All this changes the meaning of the biblical text. The way the pope renders the verse, it comes out sounding as though it supports the Mass. But in reality the pope has changed what Scripture says.

 Hebrews 9:12 indicates that Jesus "entered the holy place *once for all.*" Why does the pope render it, "*enters* into God's sanctuary*"* (present tense), as if it is still an ongoing process? Why does the pope change "*having*

obtained eternal redemption" (a past event) so that it reads "*thus obtaining* eternal redemption" (present tense)? (Emphasis added to originals.) Ask your Catholic friend about this. Then point out that not even an apostle or prophet of God would dare change what God said (see Galatians 1:8; John 10:35)!

The Sacrament of the Mass Does Not Appease God

✓ The bread and wine do not turn into the literal body and blood of Christ.

✓ John 6:51-55 does not support transubstantiation.

✓ The doctrine of the Mass detracts from the atonement wrought by Christ.

✓ Hebrews 9:12 does not support the Mass.

For further information on the Catholic view of the Mass, consult *Reasoning from the Scriptures with Catholics*, pages 171–209.

The Sacrament of Penance

Does Not Absolve Sins

Catholics believe that following a person's initial justification, the second aspect of justification occurs throughout life as he or she progresses in good works and merits the further grace necessary to enter eternal life. This means a person must sustain his or her new relationship with God and cooperate with the continuing grace of Christ in order to gain full and final justification, being cautious along the way not to commit a mortal sin (conscious, deliberate, serious sin), which erases grace from the soul. (Only *some* sins are mortal sins.)

Venial sins are lesser sins that can be pardoned. The word "venial" comes from the Latin term *venia,* which means "pardon" or "easily forgiven."[1] While these sins do involve a violation of God's holy law, they do not have any bearing as to whether a person goes to heaven or not. Venial sins weaken a person's spiritual vitality, thus making him or her more vulnerable to falling into deeper sin, but venial sins cannot keep one out of heaven.

Unlike venial sins, mortal sins are deadly or mortal in the sense that they virtually deplete the soul of God's sanctifying grace. "We commit *mortal sin* when we transgress a commandment of God in a serious matter, with full knowledge, and free consent of the will. Serious matter is, for example, unbelief, hatred of our neighbor, adultery, serious theft, murder, etc."[2] Just as a "clear" button removes all the numbers from the display of a calculator, so mortal sins "clear" the soul of God's sanctifying grace that comes at the moment of baptism.[3] Should a Catholic die in a state of having committed (and not dealt with) a mortal sin, that person will end up in hell.

For a person who commits such a sin, there is only one way to escape damnation in hell and find redemption—and that is found in confession of sin in the sacrament of penance. By confession to a priest, and doing acts of penance as instructed by the priest, a person is absolved of his sins. At that point, grace is restored to the soul.

In the sacrament of penance, the priest and confessing parishioner go through a set ritual in which each verbalizes responses and prayers. In the course of this ritual, the parishioner verbally confesses his sins, admits how often they occurred, and acknowledges sorrow for such moral failure. Following this, the parishioner is assigned some acts of penance and is instructed to say an "Act of Contrition"—a penitential prayer that indicates personal sorrow for the sins committed. The priest then typically extends his right hand toward the parishioner and absolves him of his sins. To *absolve* means "to release from the consequences of guilt."

Act of Contrition

"O my God, I am heartily sorry for having offended You. And I detest all my sins because of Your just punishment, but most of all because they offend You, my God, who are all good and deserving of all my love. I firmly resolve with the help of Your grace to confess my sins, to do penance, and to amend my life. Amen."

The parishioner then engages in "acts of penance" assigned by the priest—a typical one involves praying ten "Our Fathers" and ten "Hail Marys." He sits in the pew until this task is completed. Following this, he goes home thinking all is well with his soul. He goes home with the conviction that sanctifying grace has been restored to his soul and that he has been reconciled to God. His slate has been wiped clean—for the time being.

Penance: The Roman Catholic View

- A "venial sin" is a lesser sin that is pardonable. It does not erase grace from the soul.

- A "mortal sin" is deadly in the sense that it depletes the soul of sanctifying grace.

- Through the sacrament of penance, grace is restored to the participant's soul.

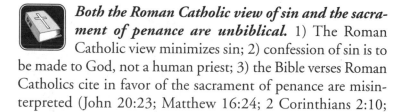

Both the Roman Catholic view of sin and the sacrament of penance are unbiblical. 1) The Roman Catholic view minimizes sin; 2) confession of sin is to be made to God, not a human priest; 3) the Bible verses Roman Catholics cite in favor of the sacrament of penance are misinterpreted (John 20:23; Matthew 16:24; 2 Corinthians 2:10; Luke 13:3).

The Roman Catholic view minimizes sin. Catholics believe that at the moment of baptism a person is cleansed of original sin and infused with sanctifying grace. This allegedly renders the person acceptable to God. At this moment the person is considered "born again." Even infants who get baptized, though completely unaware of what is going on around them, are viewed as born again and a part of God's family. These infants then grow up thinking they have *already been made right with God* by virtue of their baptism.

Their sin problem has already been taken care of (except in the event they commit a mortal sin).

The Bible, however, indicates that baptism does not save anyone, but rather takes place *after* a person has become a Christian (Acts 2:41; 8:13; 18:8). A person is "born again" the moment he or she places personal faith in Jesus Christ (John 3:1-5; Titus 3:5). A parent cannot make that decision on a child's behalf. It is something that each person must do for him- or herself, realizing that he or she is a sinner in need of redemption (see John 1:12,13).

Another problem is this: If a person grows up thinking that most of his sins have been venial sins, he may view himself as basically a good person. He may not see himself as being in dire need of a Savior. Even if that person does commit a mortal sin, the solution involves a quick trip to a priest to participate in the sacrament of penance. Easy enough. The slate is wiped clean all over again.

The Bible makes *no such distinction* between mortal and venial sins. It is true that some sins are worse than others (Proverbs 6:16-19). But never does Scripture say that only certain kinds of sin lead to spiritual death. From a biblical perspective *all sin is deadly*. Indeed, the penalty for "sin" (not just "mortal sin," but *all* sin) includes both spiritual and physical death (Romans 3:23; 6:23; 7:13). Death means "separation." Spiritual death involves spiritual separation from God. Physical death results from spiritual death, and involves separation of the soul from the body. After Adam and Eve sinned, both they and their descendants experienced spiritual separation from God, and they eventually died physically (Romans 5:12).

 Ask your Catholic friend a few questions: Did you know there is not a single reference in the Bible to "mortal sins" and "venial sins"? (Encourage him not to take your word for it, but to check it out himself.) Did you know the Bible teaches that *all* sins—not just mortal sins—cause spiritual death (that is, spiritual separation from God)?

 Some Catholics may try to argue that 1 John 5:16 supports the distinction between mortal and venial sins. This verse makes reference to "a sin that does not lead to death." This must be a venial sin. Other sins—*mortal sins*—lead to death. Actually, though, this verse does not deny that all sin leads to *spiritual* death. It simply deals with the reality that Christians can commit such horrendous sins that God judges them with premature *physical* death (see 1 Corinthians 11:30 for an example). *Ultimately* all sin leads to both spiritual and physical death. But not all sin leads to *premature* physical death.

The apostle Paul stressed that *all* human beings—not just those who commit so-called mortal sins—fall short of God's glory (Romans 3:23). The word "fall short" is a single word in the Greek and is in the present tense. This indicates continuing action. Human beings perpetually fall short of God's glory. The word "glory" here refers not just to God's splendor but to the outward manifestation of His attributes—including His righteousness, justice, and holiness. Human beings fall short of God in these and other areas.

The seriousness of man's sin problem comes into clearest focus in the words of Jesus. He taught that as a result of the fall humans are evil (Matthew 12:34) and that man is capable of great wickedness (Mark 7:20-23). Moreover, He said that man is utterly lost (Luke 19:10), that he is a sinner (Luke 15:10), that he is in need of repentance before a holy God (Mark 1:15), and that all people are indebted to and guilty before God (Luke 7:37-48).

Jesus also made it clear that both inner thoughts and external acts render a person guilty (Matthew 5:28). He taught that from within the human heart come evil thoughts, sexual immorality, theft, murder, adultery, greed, malice, deceit, envy, slander, arrogance, and folly (Mark 7:21-23). Moreover, He affirmed that God is aware of every person's sins, both external acts and inner thoughts; nothing escapes His notice (Matthew 22:18; Luke 6:8; John 4:17-19).

It is in view of the horrific nature of sin that the wonder of the salvation provided in Jesus Christ comes into clearest focus. Scripture indicates that sinners who come to Christ and place their faith in Him and Him alone are recipients of the most wonderful gift in the world—the gift of eternal salvation (Ephesians 2:8,9). The transaction is permanent. A person does not lose this gift and then have to regain it by continual visits to a priest. *It is a gift forever.* This is the glorious good news of the gospel (Luke 7:47-50; 18:9-14; Acts 10:43; Romans 3:25,28,30; 8:33,34; Galatians 4:21–5:12; 1 John 1:7–2:2).

Confession of sin is to be made to God, not a human priest. When we as Christians sin, the Holy Spirit convicts us and we experience a genuine sense of conviction that Scripture calls a "godly sorrow" (2 Corinthians 7:8-11). This leads to a sense of guilt, a sense of estrangement from God. What do we do when the Holy Spirit convicts us of sin?

Scripture says we need to confess that sin not to a priest but to God (1 John 1:9). The Greek word for *confess* literally means "to say the same thing." When I confess my sin to God, that means I am saying the same thing about my sin that God says about it. I am agreeing with God that I did wrong. No excuses! Following my confession, I can thank God that I am forgiven, because Jesus paid for my sin at the cross (2 Corinthians 5:21; Colossians 2:14). Instantly my fellowship with the Father is restored. My goal from that point forward is to walk in the power of the Holy Spirit so I will be able to resist such sins in the future (Galatians 5:22,23).

 Help your Catholic friend understand the biblical teaching that our confession is to be to *God alone*. Point out that after committing adultery with Bathsheba, David made confession directly to God: "I acknowledged my sin to you and did not cover up my iniquity. I said, 'I will confess my transgressions to the LORD'—and you forgave the guilt of my sin" (Psalm 32:5 NIV; see also Nehemiah 1:4-11; Daniel 9:3-19; Ezra 9:5-10). This same pattern of direct access to God is seen in the New Testament. Hebrews 4:16 exhorts us: "Let us therefore draw near with confidence to the throne of grace, that we may receive mercy and may find grace to help in time of need." *We do not need a priest as an intermediary.*

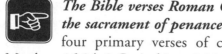 Some Catholics may point you to James 5:16, where we are told to confess our sins to *one another*. In context, this confession has nothing to do with our forgiveness before God but rather is the type that brings reconciliation among Christians who have been at odds with one another. Confessing our sins to others also makes it possible for us Christians to pray more intelligently for each other. This verse does not support the idea of making confession to a priest.

The Bible verses Roman Catholics cite in favor of the sacrament of penance are misinterpreted. The four primary verses of concern are John 20:23; Matthew 16:24; 2 Corinthians 2:10; and Luke 13:3.

John 20:23 does not support confession to a priest. Here we read, "If you forgive the sins of any, their sins have been forgiven them; if you retain the sins of any, they have been retained." Although Catholics interpret this as meaning that Christ transferred the authority to forgive sins to the apostles and their successors, the immediate and broader contexts of this verse make such a view impossible. This verse is translated more literally from the Greek as follows: "Those whose sins you forgive *have already been* forgiven; those whose sins you do not forgive *have not been* forgiven." The verse carries the idea, not that the apostles have the power to forgive sins in themselves, but that they are proclaiming what heaven *has already* proclaimed regarding forgiveness.

There is no dispute that the disciples to whom Christ was speaking were given the power to pronounce the forgiveness or retaining of sins. But all this means is that they were given the authority to *declare* what God does in regard to salvation when a person either accepts or rejects Jesus as Savior. In reality, only God can forgive sin (Mark 2:7; Luke 7:48,49). The disciples (and by extension, all believers) only have the prerogative of announcing to others that if they trust in Christ, their sins will be forgiven; if they reject Christ as Savior, their sins will not be forgiven. We have the authority to make that declaration because God Himself has already declared it in heaven. As His representatives, we declare to others what He has already declared.

 Show your Catholic friend that in the book of Acts we never witness the apostles themselves explicitly forgiving others' sins. Rather, we witness them proclaiming God's forgiveness of sin based on belief in Christ as Savior (for example, Acts 5:31; 10:43; 13:38; 26:18). They merely announced what heaven had *already* announced.

There is no statement in the text of Scripture to the effect that only validly ordained priests were to possess the power to announce the forgiveness of sins. All the early believers proclaimed the gospel by which sins are forgiven (Romans 1:16; 1 Corinthians 15:1-4). Even Philip, who was only a deacon (Acts 6:5), and not an elder or priest (in the Roman Catholic sense), preached the gospel to the Samaritans (Acts 8:5).

Matthew 16:24 does not support the need for penitential works. Jesus said to His disciples, 'If anyone wishes to come after Me, he must deny himself, and take up his cross and follow Me.'" Some Catholics say Jesus' instruction here refers to the necessity of doing penitential works (acts of penance in the sacrament of penance).[4]

Contextually, this verse refers not to doing penitential works (which Roman Catholics typically say are necessary for salvation), but rather refers to the life of commitment of a person who has *already become saved.* Christ is calling on those who have already trusted in Him for salvation to totally commit themselves to living for Him daily.

These words of Jesus would certainly have made sense to His first-century hearers, since the cross was a quite common tool of execution. When a man had been condemned to die, and the time of execution had arrived, the man would be required by the Roman executioners to carry his own cross to the place of execution. This is much as it was with Jesus when the time of His execution came (John 19:17).

As we "take up" our "cross" and follow Jesus, we are willingly submitting ourselves to Him. Jesus is calling for a total commitment. The idea is this: "If you really want to follow Me, do not do so in word only, but put your life on the line and follow Me on the path of the cross—a path that may involve sacrifice, suffering, and possibly even death."

When Jesus instructed those listening to Him to take up their crosses and "follow" Him, He used a present imperative form of the word "follow." This is highly significant. The present tense indicates continuous action, the imperative indicates a command. We are to perpetually and unceasingly follow Jesus, day in and day out. But acts of penance are nowhere in view.

Second Corinthians 2:10 does not support priests absolving sins. The apostle Paul writes here, "One whom you forgive anything, I forgive also; for indeed what I have forgiven, if I have forgiven anything, I did it for your sakes in the presence of Christ." Catholic theologians say that in this verse we find the apostle Paul exercising the power of absolution given to him by Christ. Christ likewise "promised to His Church and transmitted to His Church the power to forgive sins without limitation."[5]

Contextually, however, this verse has nothing to do with exercising the power of absolution. Rather it deals with an incident of discipline in the church of Corinth. The person of whom Paul was speaking had committed a serious offense, and as a result severe church discipline was imposed upon him. Paul now urged the Corinthian believers to lovingly restore this person to fellowship in view of the remorse the person had shown. The person had repented, and hence forgiveness was in order. After all, the purpose of church discipline is to restore a person to fellowship, not to permanently injure him.

It was in this context that Paul said, "One whom you forgive anything, I forgive also; for indeed what I have forgiven, if I have forgiven anything, I did it for your sakes in the presence of Christ." He then indicated it was important for the offender to be restored so the incident would not become an occasion for Satan to drive a wedge between the church and Paul (verse 11).

Many scholars believe that in this verse Paul was personally forgiving an offense *directed at him,* and then urging the Corinthian believers to forgive the person and restore him to fellowship. If this is correct, as the evidence seems to indicate, Paul in verse 10 is simply saying that he has already forgiven the man in question, if, in fact, there was anything to forgive in the first place. Paul was taking the initiative in forgiveness, then making sure the Corinthians followed suit. Seen in this light, the verse cannot be used to support the Roman Catholic view of a priest absolving people from their sins. *Paul was expressing personal forgiveness.*

 Since the context indicates that an individual who had personally and publicly attacked Paul had repented after being disciplined by the Corinthian church, does it not make sense that Paul would want to verbalize his *personal* forgiveness of the offender to the Corinthians? When Paul's words are seen in this light, priestly absolution of sin is nowhere in view. Help your Catholic friend understand the context of this passage.

Luke 13:3 does not support penance. A Catholic translation of this verse reads, "The Lord also said: 'Except you do penance, you shall all likewise perish.'" Catholics say this verse supports the sacrament of penance.[6]

To put it plainly, the Catholic translation of this verse is incorrect. The Greek word in question, *metanoe,* means "to change one's mind," "to repent."[7] The phrase in question should be translated, "Unless you *repent,* you will all likewise perish" (New American Standard Version, emphasis added), not "Except you do *penance,* you shall all likewise perish" (Roman Catholic translation, emphasis added). Obviously there is a big difference between the sacrament of penance and a call to repentance.

Contextually, in Luke 13:1 we find the account of some Galileans who had been slain by Pilate's soldiers while offering sacrifices at the Temple so that their blood and that of the sacrifices were mixed. Christ's subsequent point in verses 2 and 3 is that this horrible thing did not happen to them because they were worse sinners than all other Galileans, but that *all* people are sinners and need to repent. Death is a common denominator for the whole human race. Only repentance can bring life; only repentance can prepare people to enter into God's holy kingdom. "Unless you repent, you will all likewise perish." *Penance is nowhere in view here.*

The Sacrament of Penance Does Not Absolve Sins

✓ The Roman Catholic view minimizes sin. *All* sin separates us from God.

✓ Confession of sin is to be made to God, not a human priest.

✓ The Bible verses Roman Catholics cite in favor of the sacrament of penance are misinterpreted.

For further information on the Catholic view of penance, consult *Reasoning from the Scriptures with Catholics*, pages 211–31.

9

There Is No Purgatory,

Nor Is It Needed

The *Catechism of the Catholic Church* tells us that "all who die in God's grace and friendship, but still imperfectly purified, are indeed assured of their eternal salvation; but after death they undergo purification, so as to achieve the holiness necessary to enter the joy of heaven."[1] This purification takes place in purgatory.

Catholics believe that the temporal punishments of sins committed before baptism are remitted by the sacrament of baptism. If a person sins *after* baptism, however, even when these sins are forgiven (in terms of *eternal* punishment in hell) through the sacrament of penance, *the temporal punishments remain.* These punishments can be expiated (or compensated for) by penitential works in this life, or in the future (following death) in purgatory. Matthew 5:26 allegedly indicates that *every last ounce* ("up to the last cent") of temporal punishment must be paid.

The Purpose of Purgatory

"The purpose of purgatory is to cleanse one of imperfections, venial sins, and faults, and to remit or do away with the temporal punishment due to mortal sins that have been forgiven in the Sacrament of Penance" *(Pocket Catholic Dictionary).*

To most Catholics, purgatory makes good sense—especially in the context of a works-oriented system of salvation. After all, most people seem to have an intuitive awareness that they have done enough bad things in life that they really do not deserve to spend eternity in heaven. Seen in this way, a little punishment for the wrongs committed in this life is not viewed as unreasonable for those on the road to heaven. Purgatory meets this need. Of course, because people have varying levels of sin in their lives, they spend varying amounts of time in purgatory before going to heaven.

Catholics believe that, if you have loved ones in purgatory, there are things you can do to shorten their stay there. For example, you can say prayers, and give alms, and perform good works. All these are viewed as meritorious, and can aid a soul in purgatory. But if you really want to help your loved one, you can ask the priest to say a Mass on his or her behalf.

Closely related to the doctrine of purgatory is the doctrine of indulgences. The Roman Catholic Church teaches that the church is the steward of a vast reservoir of merit, called the "Treasury of Merit." This treasury was allegedly filled up by the works and prayers of Jesus Christ, His mother Mary, and the saints of all ages. The treasury of merit is so vast that it can never be exhausted or depleted. The Roman Catholic church allegedly has the power to dispense from this reservoir "indulgences," which are said to cancel the debt of temporal punishment.

Once one has gained an indulgence, one can apply it either to oneself (thereby reducing one's own temporal punishment for sins committed), or one can by prayer apply it to the account of a dead loved one believed to be in purgatory. So, indulgences can benefit both oneself and one's dead loved ones.[2]

What kinds of things must one do to gain an indulgence? One of the most common is making the sign of the cross (which grants a partial indulgence of three years less time in purgatory). Reciting the Rosary in a family group can grant an indulgence of ten years.[3] Visiting a Catholic shrine can also grant an indulgence. To gain a *plenary* indulgence (an indulgence that cancels *all* the temporal punishment a person has accumulated), three additional conditions must be met: sacramental confession, Eucharistic communion, and prayer for the pope.

Purgatory: The Roman Catholic View

- Purgatory is a place where the soul is purged and readied for life in heaven.

- People spend varying amounts of time in purgatory, depending on the level of purging needed.

- A person can shorten a loved one's stay in purgatory by prayers, alms, and good works.

- There is a Treasury of Merit earned by the works and prayers of Jesus, Mary, and the saints.

- The church can dispense "indulgences" from this treasury to shorten a person's stay in purgatory.

The Bible indicates there is no such thing as purgatory, and the very idea of such a place devalues the redemption provided by Christ. 1) Purgatory contradicts the "good news of the gospel" of which Scripture speaks; 2) purgatory is an outgrowth of Roman Catholicism's weak view of justification; 3) Jesus' work on the cross makes purgatory unnecessary; 4) at death believers have a single destiny—heaven; 5) the doctrine of purgatory has a connection to the occult; 6) the doctrine of indulgences is incompatible with grace; and 7) the Bible verses Catholics cite in favor of purgatory and indulgences are misinterpreted.

Purgatory contradicts the "good news of the gospel" of which Scripture speaks. Consider what Catholics are saying in regard to purgatory. Let's say you are a good-hearted Catholic, and you do all the things required by your church throughout life. You regularly attend Mass, you work hard to maintain sanctifying grace in your soul by being faithful, and you confess your sins to a priest when you do wrong. You are always careful to participate in the sacrament of penance after committing what you think may be a mortal sin. You do all this, *and more,* in keeping with what your church tells you. When you die, *you will likely still have to go to purgatory before being granted entrance into heaven.* Throughout your lifetime you could attend over a thousand Masses and still die not fully purified from sin. This is *not* the "good news" of the gospel of grace spoken of in the New Testament, "for it is by grace you have been saved, through faith—and this not from yourselves, it is the gift of God—not by works, so that no one can boast" (Ephesians 2:8,9 NIV)!

 Purgatory is an outgrowth of Roman Catholicism's weak view of justification. Since only perfectly righteous people get into heaven, and since in the Roman Catholic view of justification a person is *not* absolutely and once-for-all declared righteous by God, then somehow a person must *become* perfectly righteous before entrance into heaven is granted. This happens via purgatory (among other things). Contrary to the Catholic view, the biblical view of justification involves a singular and instantaneous event in which God declares the believing sinner to be righteous (Romans 3:24,28— see chapter 6 for more on justification).

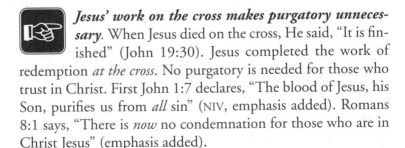 ***Jesus' work on the cross makes purgatory unnecessary.*** When Jesus died on the cross, He said, "It is finished" (John 19:30). Jesus completed the work of redemption *at the cross.* No purgatory is needed for those who trust in Christ. First John 1:7 declares, "The blood of Jesus, his Son, purifies us from *all* sin" (NIV, emphasis added). Romans 8:1 says, "There is *now* no condemnation for those who are in Christ Jesus" (emphasis added).

We are cleansed not by the "fire of purgatory" but by the blood of Jesus (Hebrews 9:14). Jesus "Himself is the propitiation for our sins" (1 John 2:2). It is through Jesus' work on the cross that we are made righteous (2 Corinthians 5:21). The apostle Paul spoke of himself as "not having a righteousness of my own derived from the Law, but that which is through faith in Christ, the righteousness which comes from God on the basis of faith" (Philippians 3:9). It is through this wonderful work of Christ on the cross that believers are "blameless," and hence they have no need of an imagined purgatory (Jude 1:24; see also Ephesians 1:4).

A key verse to share with your Catholic friend is Hebrews 10:14: "By one offering He has *perfected for all time* those who are sanctified" (emphasis added). No further purging is necessary because Christ has perfected "for all time" those who have believed in Him. *That which is already perfect "for all time" needs no further purging.*

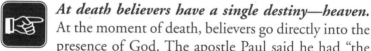

At death believers have a single destiny—heaven. At the moment of death, believers go directly into the presence of God. The apostle Paul said he had "the desire to depart and be with Christ, for that is very much better" (Philippians 1:23). Paul knew that the very moment after he physically died, he would be with Christ in heaven. He knew that "to be absent from the body" is to be "at home with the Lord." We read in 2 Corinthians 5:6-8: "Being always of good courage, and knowing that while we are at home in the body we are absent from the Lord—for we walk by faith, not by sight— we are of good courage, I say, and prefer rather to be absent from the body and to be at home with the Lord."

In the phrase, "be at home *with* the Lord," the Greek word *pros* is used for "with." This word suggests very close, face-to-face fellowship. It is a word used of intimate relationships. Paul thereby indicates that the fellowship he expects to have with Christ immediately following his physical death will be one of great intimacy.

In view of such verses, there is clearly no stop-off at purgatory for believers who die. Rather, the instant they die, all believers are ushered directly into the presence of Christ.

 How can the teaching of Philippians 1:23 and 2 Corinthians 5:8 that all believers in Christ go *straight to heaven* at the moment of death be reconciled with the Catholic doctrine of purgatory? Be sure to ask your Catholic friend about this.

The doctrine of purgatory has a connection to the occult. Researchers John Ankerberg and John Weldon have noted an occult connection to the doctrine of purgatory. They observe that throughout the history of the Roman Catholic Church there have been widespread reports of apparitions alleged to be those of dead persons:

> As an example we could cite *The Dogma of Purgatory,* containing both Catholic seals of approval (the *nihil obstat* and *imprimatur*), signifying a book is "free of doctrinal or moral error." This book is full of stories of the alleged spirits of deceased Catholics appearing to the faithful and warning them of the torments of purgatory. The result? Inevitably it is a greater bonding to Roman Catholic beliefs and practice.[4]

This is nothing less than spiritism. And all forms of spiritism are condemned by God as heinous sin. Deuteronomy 18:10-12 is clear: "Let no one be found among you who...consults the dead. Anyone who does these things is detestable to the LORD."

The doctrine of indulgences is incompatible with grace. As is the case with the doctrine of purgatory, the Roman Catholic practice of indulgences is an outgrowth of the insufficient Roman Catholic view of justification. Because the church has offered a view of justification that is lacking, it presents many little Band-Aid fixes—including indulgences—to help the believer on his or her road to salvation.

Consider the logical implications of this doctrine. A person must not only do meritorious works throughout life to help earn salvation, but must then suffer for a time in purgatory after death. His surviving loved ones can then do good works and gain indulgences to help shorten his time in purgatory. How can it be argued that this is not a works-oriented view of salvation?

The doctrine of indulgences certainly compromises the atonement wrought by Christ at the cross. If the doctrine of indulgences is true, this means that Christ did not accomplish *full* redemption at the cross. He got only part of the job done. Biblically, though, Christ *did* get the job done (see 2 Corinthians 5:19-21), and the Bible tells us that the sins of those who trust in Christ are fully forgiven: "When you were dead in your transgressions and the uncircumcision of your flesh, He made you alive together with Him, *having forgiven us all our transgressions*" (Colossians 2:13, emphasis added—see also Romans 3:25,28,30; 8:33,34).

Romans 3:24 tells us that God's declaration of righteousness is given to believers "freely by his grace" (NIV). The word *grace* literally means "unmerited favor." It is because of God's unmerited favor that believers can freely be "declared righteous" before God. *Indulgences (earned by merit) play no role!* One will look in vain in Scripture for a single explicit reference to indulgences. Emphasize this point to your Catholic friend.

Some Catholics may try to argue for indulgences from Galatians 6:2, where the apostle Paul instructs us to "bear one another's burdens, and thereby fulfill the law of Christ."[5] A look at the context, however, indicates that Paul is not saying we can bear the *punishment* for someone else's sin. After all, just two verses later Paul reminds us that "whatever a man sows, this he will also reap" (verse 7). The "burdens" Paul refers to are not *sins* but rather the *problems* all of us face from time to time. The spirit of the verse is this: "When life throws your brother or sister a punch, help him or her in any way you can."

The Greek word for "burdens" carries the idea of "weights." Often weights can exceed the strength of the person trying to do the lifting and overwhelm the person to the point of giving up. So it is with life's problems. Sometimes they get too heavy to bear. That is why Paul says we should help others carry their load in life. By doing this, we fulfill the law of Christ, namely, "love" (see Galatians 5:14).

 The Bible verses Catholics cite in favor of purgatory and indulgences are misinterpreted.

First Corinthians 3:10-15. In this passage we read:

> According to the grace of God which was given to me, like a wise master builder I laid a foundation, and another is building upon it. But each man must be careful how he builds on it. For no man can lay a foundation other than the one which is laid, which is Jesus Christ. Now if any man builds upon the foundation with gold, silver, precious stones, wood, hay, straw, each man's work will become evident; for the day will show it because it is to be revealed with fire; and the fire itself will test the quality of each man's work. If any man's work which he has built upon it remains, he will receive a reward. If any man's work is burned up, he will suffer loss; but he himself will be saved, yet so as through fire.

Though Catholics interpret this as referring to purgatory,[6] this doctrine is nowhere to be found in the context. This passage indicates that the believer's *works* will be tested by fire at the Judgment Seat of Christ, not that the believer himself will be purged by fire. That is an entirely different thing. The verse speaks of the receiving or losing of rewards based on works done on earth *after one has trusted in Christ and has been saved.* If the saved person's works withstand the fire, they will receive an eternal reward. If the saved person's works do not withstand the fire, they will not receive a reward. Either way, the person is still saved, even if his works should be burned up (verse 15).

 There is a big difference between purging a *person* of sin (the Catholic view) and testing a *person's works* to determine if they are worthy of reward (Paul's statement in 1 Corinthians 3:10-15). Help your Catholic friend understand that since this passage is talking about *rewards* for faithfulness and *loss of rewards* for a lack of faithfulness, purgatory is nowhere in view.

The first letter to the Corinthians was written "to those who have been sanctified in Christ Jesus" (1 Corinthians 1:2). These individuals were already in full possession of salvation. No further purging was necessary for them, for all their sins had already been purged from them by Christ at the cross. They were secure in their salvation (see Ephesians 4:30 and Romans 8:29,30).

Matthew 12:32. Jesus says here, "Whoever speaks a word against the Son of Man, it shall be forgiven him; but whoever speaks against the Holy Spirit, it shall not be forgiven him, either in this age *or in the age to come*" (emphasis added). Catholics sometimes reason that if certain sins like blasphemy against the Holy Spirit *cannot* be forgiven in the "age to come," then other sins *may* be forgiven in the "age to come"[7] (that is, via purgatory).

When Jesus says the sin against the Holy Spirit will not be forgiven in this age or the "age to come," this is simply a Jewish idiomatic way of saying the sin will *never* be forgiven. This becomes clear in the parallel account in Mark 3:29: "Whoever blasphemes against the Holy Spirit *never has forgiveness, but is guilty of an eternal sin*" (emphasis added). Hence, there is no support for the Catholic doctrine of purgatory in these verses.

The broader backdrop to understanding Matthew 12:32 is that the Jews who had just witnessed a mighty miracle should have recognized that Jesus had performed it in the power of the Holy Spirit. After all, the Hebrew Scriptures, with which the Jews were well acquainted, prophesied that when the Messiah came He would perform certain mighty miracles in the power of the Spirit—like giving sight to the blind, opening deaf ears, and enabling the lame to walk (see Isaiah 35:5,6). Instead, these Jewish leaders claimed that Christ did these miracles in the power of the devil, the *un*holy spirit. This was a sin against the Holy Spirit. This shows that these Jewish leaders had completely hardened themselves against the things of God.

In the context of Matthew 12, "blaspheming the Spirit" involved the Jews opposing Jesus' messiahship so firmly and definitively that they resorted to accusing Jesus of sorcery in order to avoid the impact of the Holy Spirit's miraculous signs that confirmed Christ's messianic identity. This is truly a damning sin, for there is no other provision for man's sin than the work of the one true Messiah as attested to by the Holy Spirit.

Matthew 5:26. Here we read the following words of Jesus: "Truly I say to you, you will not come out of there until you have paid up the last cent." Some Catholic theologians believe this parable lends support to the doctrine of purgatory.[8] However, this interpretation is completely foreign to the context. That Jesus is referring to a *physical* prison during earthly life and not a *spiritual* prison in the afterlife is clear from the previous verse: "Make friends quickly with your opponent at law while you are with him on the way, so that your opponent may not hand you over to the judge, and the judge to the officer, and you be thrown into prison" (verse 25). Jesus is simply giving a practical teaching about reconciliation of human conflicts and the avoidance of situations that naturally lead to anger and personal injury (see 5:21-24).

Second Corinthians 12:15. The apostle Paul wrote this to the Corinthian believers: "I will most gladly spend and be expended for your souls." Some Catholic theologians say this verse lends support to the doctrine of indulgences, by which the merits of one person can be transferred to another.

However, neither purgatory nor indulgences are mentioned or alluded to in the verse. Paul's desire to "spend and be expended" is for the Corinthians as *living* believers (see verse 14), not as dead believers in a place of suffering (purgatory). Further, Paul's suffering has nothing to do with the temporal consequences of the Corinthians' sins, but rather relates to Paul's burden to minister the grace of Christ to them (see verses 11-19). He is willing not only to spend his money but to expend *himself* on behalf of these (living) Corinthian believers whom he loved. Contextually, then, this verse cannot be cited to support the doctrine of indulgences.

There Is No Purgatory, Nor Is It Needed

✓ Purgatory contradicts the "good news of the gospel" of which Scripture speaks.

✓ Purgatory is an outgrowth of Roman Catholicism's weak view of justification.

✓ Jesus' work on the cross makes purgatory unnecessary.

✓ At death believers have a single destiny—heaven.

✓ The doctrine of purgatory has a connection to the occult.

✓ The doctrine of indulgences is incompatible with grace.

✓ The Bible verses Catholics cite in favor of purgatory and indulgences are misinterpreted.

 For further information on the Catholic view of purgatory, consult *Reasoning from the Scriptures with Catholics*, pages 233–55.

10

Jesus Has Changed My life

Forever

One of the ten most important things to say to a Catholic should be an account of what Jesus has done in your life—especially pertaining to the grace-gift of salvation He has given you. Giving your testimony—your personal story—is an important component of any witnessing encounter.

In my own case, throughout my childhood and teenage years I thought I was a Christian because I regularly attended church. For years I participated in various church activities, sang in the church choir, and went through all the motions. I did lots of Christianlike things! I even went through a confirmation ceremony at my church—an event that was supposed to *confirm* I was a Christian. I had no idea at that time that I really was not a Christian according to the biblical definition of the term.

Like so many others today, I was under the illusion that a Christian was a church-attender, or one who basically subscribed to a Christian code of ethics. I believed that as long as I was fairly consistent in living my life in accordance with this code of ethics, I was surely a Christian. I believed that as long as my good deeds outweighed my bad deeds by the time I died, I could look forward to a destiny in heaven.

It was not until years later I came to understand that the mere act of going to church did not make me a Christian. As evangelist Billy Sunday (1862–1935) put it, "Going to church doesn't make you a Christian any more than going to a garage makes you an automobile."[1]

Most fundamentally, a Christian is one who has a personal, ongoing relationship with Jesus. It is a relationship that begins the moment one places faith in Christ for salvation. It has been well said that Christianity is not so much a *religion* as it is a *relationship*.

The word "Christian" is actually used only three times in the New Testament—the most important being in Acts 11:26 (see also Acts 26:28 and 1 Peter 4:16). It is instructive to observe what this word meant among those to whom the term was originally applied. By so doing, we can see whether we are Christians according to the way the Bible itself defines the term.

In Acts 11:26, we are told simply and straightforwardly that "the disciples were first called Christians at Antioch." This would have been around A.D. 42, about a decade after Christ died on the cross and rose from the dead.

What does the term mean? The answer is found in the "ian" ending—for among the ancients this ending meant "belonging to the party of." "Herodians" belonged to the party of Herod. "Caesarians" belonged to the party of Caesar. "Christians" belonged to Christ. And Christians were loyal to Christ, just as the Herodians were loyal to Herod and Caesarians were loyal to Caesar (see Matthew 22:16; Mark 3:6; 12:13).

The significance of the name *Christian* was that these followers of Jesus were recognized as a distinct group. Their party was seen as distinct from Judaism, and as distinct from all other religions of the ancient world. We might loosely translate the term Christian as "those belonging to Christ," "Christ-ones," or perhaps "Christ-people." *They are ones who follow Christ.*

Try to imagine what it may have been like in Antioch as one local resident talked to another about these followers of Jesus: "Who are these people?" the one Antiochan might ask—and the other would reply, "Oh, these are the people who are always talking about Christ—the Christ-people, the Christians."

Scholars have noted that the Antiochans were well known for making fun of others. It may be that the early followers of Jesus were called "Christians" as a term of derision or ridicule. But history reveals that, by the second century, Christians had adopted the title as a badge of honor. They took pride (healthy pride) in following Jesus. They had a genuine relationship with the living, resurrected Christ.

I bring all this up because a pivotal part of your personal testimony to a Roman Catholic must be the fact that you are sure of going to heaven precisely because you have a personal relationship with Christ. You have meaning in your present life not because you obey rules and participate in rituals and sacraments, but because you know Jesus.

Great Christians throughout church history have always emphasized that Christianity most fundamentally involves such a personal relationship:

- Josiah Strong (1847–1916) said, "Christianity is neither a creed nor a ceremonial, but life vitally connected with a loving Christ."[2]

- John R.W. Stott (born 1921) wrote, "A Christian is, in essence, somebody personally related to Jesus Christ."[3]

- Oswald Chambers (1874–1917) said, "Christianity is not devotion to work, or to a cause, or a doctrine, but devotion to a person, the Lord Jesus Christ."[4]

- Billy Graham (born 1918) declared, "Christianity isn't only going to church on Sunday. It is living twenty-four hours of every day with Jesus Christ."[5]

Having laid this basic foundation, I now want to give you a few pointers to keep in mind in regard to testimonies. These pointers are the very things I keep in mind when I tell people what the Lord has done in my own life.

 There is a strong biblical precedent for God's people telling others about what God has done in their lives, and we are to follow the examples given in the Bible:

- "Give thanks to the LORD, call on his name; make known among the nations what he has done" (1 Chronicles 16:8 NIV).

- "Tell of all his wonderful acts" (1 Chronicles 16:9 NIV).

- "Proclaim among the nations what he has done" (Psalm 9:11 NIV).

- "Whoever acknowledges me before men, I will also acknowledge him before my Father in heaven" (Matthew 10:32 NIV).

- "Jesus…said, 'Go home to your family and tell them how much the Lord has done for you, and how he has had mercy on you.' So the man went away and began to tell in the Decapolis how much Jesus had done for him. And all the people were amazed" (Mark 5:19,20 NIV).

- "Leaving her water jar, the woman went back to the town and said to the people, 'Come, see a man who told me everything I ever did. Could this be the Christ?' They came out of the town and made their way toward him. …Many of the Samaritans from that town believed in him because of the woman's testimony, 'He told me everything I ever did'" (John 4:28-31,39 NIV).

- "Do not be ashamed to testify about our Lord" (2 Timothy 1:8 NIV).

- "Always be prepared to give an answer to everyone who asks you to give the reason for the hope that you have. But do this with gentleness and respect" (1 Peter 3:15 NIV).

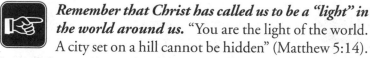

Remember that Christ has called us to be a "light" in the world around us. "You are the light of the world. A city set on a hill cannot be hidden" (Matthew 5:14). Jesus did not call us to be "secret agent" Christians. We are not to cloak our lights. Someone once said, "No one is a light unto himself, not even the sun."[6] Because of the false doctrines permeating our society, there has never been a time when the "light" of each Christian has been more needed. Billy Graham said, "The Christian should stand out like a sparkling diamond."[7]

How You Live Is Important

Keep in mind that it is not just our words that serve as a witness for Jesus. Our actions, too, serve as a witness. What we believe as Christians has an effect on the way we live. Don't just share the *facts* of your relationship with Jesus with a Roman Catholic; let him see the *effects* of that relationship in your life.

We are called to be personal witnesses about Jesus Christ specifically. Just before ascending into heaven Jesus instructed His disciples: "You will receive power when the Holy Spirit has come upon you; and you shall be My witnesses both in Jerusalem, and in all Judea and Samaria, and even to the remotest part of the earth" (Acts 1:8). A *witness* is a person who gives testimony. Christians testify *about Jesus*—who He is, what He has done, and their personal relationship with Him.

A Christian leader once said, "Every heart *with* Christ is a missionary; every heart *without* Christ is a mission field." We can be missionaries to Catholics when we encounter them in day-to-day living. We must always be ready to share the gospel of grace with them.

 When you tell others what the Lord has done in your life, speak with conviction. You may not be an authority about what every single verse in the Bible says, but you *are* an authority on what Jesus has personally done in your life. In our day of relativism—a day in which there is so much confusion about so many things—a testimony delivered with conviction will be noticed (see Acts 2:32; 3:15; 4:33; 13:30,31).

 Be careful not to have a "spiritual chip" on your shoulder when you give your testimony. A "spiritual chip" is the communication of the feeling that you are looking down on the Catholic because you have something he or she does not have. Such an attitude will turn him or her off as fast as anything you can imagine.[8]

Especially for Christians who have thoroughly prepared themselves by learning hard-hitting scriptural answers to Catholic doctrinal errors, the temptation may be to *talk down* to the Catholic instead of *conversing with* the Catholic. Do not let this happen. Be on your guard and make every effort, with God's help, to remain humble during your witnessing encounter. Watch out for spiritual pride; it is deadly!

 When giving your testimony, be sure to share what your life was like **before *you were a Christian*, how *you became a Christian, and what your life has been like* since *becoming a Christian*.**

• Describe what your life was like before you were a Christian. What were your feelings, attitudes, actions, and relationships like during this time? (The apostle Paul clearly spoke of what his life was like before he was a Christian in Acts 26:4-11.)

- What events happened in your life that led you to your decision to trust in Christ? What caused you to begin considering Christ as a solution to your needs? Was there a crisis? A lack of meaning in life? Be specific.

- Describe your conversion experience. Was it a book you read? Were you in a church? Were other Christians with you at the time? (The apostle Paul straightforwardly told how he became a Christian in Acts 26:12-18.)

- What kind of change took place in your life following your conversion? What effect did trusting in Christ have on your feelings, attitudes, actions, and relationships? (Paul spoke of how his life changed once he became a Christian in Acts 26:19-23.)

 There are certain things you should avoid when sharing your personal testimony:

- *Do not be long-winded.* People have short attention spans. Unless they indicate they want every detail, try to cover the essential points briefly.

- *Try not to use "Christianese" language.* In other words, do not use too much theological language your listener may be unfamiliar with. If you do use theological words or "Christian" expressions that are not everyday language, be sure to clearly define what you mean by them.

- *Do not communicate in your testimony that true Christianity yields a bed of roses for believers.* Such a claim is simply not true. You might even share some of the struggles you have gone through since becoming a Christian. Your listener may identify with what you have gone through.

- *Do not be insensitive to the Catholic's "works" background.*
The apostle Paul in 1 Corinthians 2:14 stated: "A natural
man does not accept the things of the Spirit of God, for
they are foolishness to him; and he cannot understand
them, because they are spiritually appraised." The gospel
of God's grace may not make much sense to a person who
has been thoroughly schooled in the necessity of works.
For this reason, devote a good part of your testimony to
how the gospel of God's grace has set you free.

 ***As you finish your testimony, leave the Roman
Catholic with a clear picture of how to become a
Christian.*** Here are the most important points:

1. *God Desires a Personal Relationship with Human Beings*
God created human beings (Genesis 1:27). And He did not
just create them to exist all alone and apart from Him. He created them so that they might come into a personal relationship
with Him. God had face-to-face encounters and fellowship with
Adam and Eve, the first couple (Genesis 3:8-19). Just as God
fellowshipped with them, so He desires to fellowship *with us*
(1 John 1:5-7). God *loves* us (John 3:16).
The problem is . . .

2.*Humanity Has a Sin Problem that Blocks a Relationship
with God*
When Adam and Eve chose to sin against God, they cata-
pulted the entire human race—to which they gave birth—into
sin. Since the time of Adam and Eve, every human being has
been born into the world with a propensity to sin. The apostle
Paul affirmed that "sin entered the world through one man, and
death through sin" (Romans 5:12 NIV).
Jesus often spoke of sin in metaphors that illustrate the havoc
it wreaks in one's life. He described sin as *blindness* (Matthew
23:16-26), *sickness* (Matthew 9:12), being *enslaved in bondage*

(John 8:34), and *living in darkness* (John 8:12; 12:35-46). Moreover, Jesus taught that these are *universal conditions* and that all people are guilty before God (Luke 7:37-48).

Of course, some people are more morally upright than others. (The Catholic to whom you are speaking may well be highly moral.) But even if we try to live a life of consistent good works, *we all fall short of God's infinite standards* (Romans 3:23). In a contest to see who can throw a rock to the moon, I am sure a muscular athlete would be able to throw the rock much further than I could. But all humans fall far short of the task. Similarly, all of us fall short of measuring up to God's perfect holy standards.

Though the problem is a serious one, God has graciously provided a solution:

3. Jesus Died for Our Sins and Made Salvation Possible

God's absolute holiness demands that sin be punished. The good news of the gospel, however, is that Jesus has taken this punishment *entirely* on Himself. God loves us so much that He sent Jesus to bear the entire penalty for our sins!

It is critical that you help your Catholic friend understand what Scripture says about this. Jesus affirmed that it was for the very purpose of dying that He came into the world (John 12:27). Moreover, He declared that His death was a sacrificial offering for the sins of humanity (Matthew 26:26-28). Jesus took His sacrificial mission with utmost seriousness, for He knew that without Him, humanity would certainly perish (Matthew 16:25; John 3:16) and spend eternity apart from God in a place of great suffering (Matthew 10:28; 11:23; 23:33; 25:41; Luke 16:22-28). Jesus therefore described His mission this way: "The Son of Man did not come to be served, but to serve, and to give his life a ransom for many" (Matthew 20:28).

4. *Faith in Jesus Is Required*

By His sacrificial death on the cross, Jesus took the sins of the entire world on Himself and made salvation available to everyone (1 John 2:2). But this salvation is not automatic. Only those who choose to believe in Christ are saved. This is the consistent testimony of the biblical Jesus. "God so loved the world that he gave his one and only Son, that whoever *believes* in him shall not perish but have eternal life." "I am the resurrection and the life; he who *believes* in me will live even if he dies" (John 3:16; 11:25 NIV, emphasis added). Faith in Christ is what brings salvation, not meritorious works and participation in Roman Catholic sacraments.

Choosing not to believe in Jesus, by contrast, leads to eternal condemnation: "Whoever believes in him is not condemned, but whoever *does not believe* stands condemned already because he has not believed in the name of God's one and only Son" (John 3:18 NIV, emphasis added).

5. *We Are Free at Last: Forgiven of All Sins*

When a person believes in Christ, a wonderful thing happens. God forgives him of all his sins. *All of them!* He puts them completely out of His sight. A person doesn't lose salvation or justification because he or she commits a "mortal sin." Be sure to share the following verses, which speak of the total forgiveness of those who have believed in Christ:

- "In him we have redemption through his blood, the forgiveness of sins, in accordance with the riches of God's grace" (Ephesians 1:7 NIV).

- "Their sins and lawless acts I will remember no more" (Hebrews 10:17 NIV).

- "Blessed is he whose transgressions are forgiven, whose sins are covered. Blessed is the man whose sin the LORD does not count against him and in whose spirit is no deceit" (Psalm 32:1,2 NIV).

- "As far as the east is from the west, so far has He removed our transgressions from us" (Psalm 103:12).

Such forgiveness is wonderful indeed, for—despite what the Roman Catholic Church says—none of us can possibly gain "final justification" by meritorious works, or be good enough to warrant God's favor. Because of what Jesus has done for us, we freely receive the gift of salvation. It is a gift provided solely through the grace of God (Ephesians 2:8,9). And all of it is ours by simply believing in Jesus.

6. *Don't Put It Off*

Help your Catholic friend see that it is a dangerous thing to put off turning to Christ alone for salvation, for no one knows the day of his or her death. What if it happens this evening? "Death is the destiny of every man; the living should take this to heart" (Ecclesiastes 7:2 NIV). "Seek the LORD while He may be found; call upon Him while He is near" (Isaiah 55:6).

7. *Pray a Simple Prayer of Faith*

If the Catholic to whom you are speaking expresses interest in trusting in *Jesus alone* who provides a salvation through *grace alone* by *faith alone,* lead him or her in a simple prayer. Be sure to emphasize that it is not prayer that saves anyone. It is the *faith in one's heart* that brings salvation. The following prayer is just a simple expression of this:

> *Dear Jesus,*
> *I want to have a relationship with You.*
> *I know I can't save myself by meritorious works,*
> *because I'm a sinner.*
> *Thank You for dying on the cross on my behalf.*
> *I believe You died for me, and I accept Your free gift of salvation.*
> *Thank You, Jesus.*
> *Amen.*

8. *Welcome the Roman Catholic into God's Forever Family*

On the authority of the Word of God, you can now assure your Catholic friend that he or she is a part of God's forever family. Encourage him or her with the prospect of spending all eternity by the side of Jesus in heaven!

 For further information on witnessing to Catholics, consult *Reasoning from the Scriptures with Catholics*, pages 11–22 and 323–28.

 An Exhortation: The Catholic you have led to Christ still needs your help! Get him grounded in a good Bible-believing church. Introduce him to some of your Christian friends, and have your friends pray for him regularly. Realize that he may be carrying some psychological and spiritual "baggage" from his past association with Roman Catholicism—especially in regard to the issue of meritorious works. Nurture him or her along in what it means to live day-by-day under God's wonderful grace.

Be sensitive to the fact that your friend's family members may not only resist but become very angry over this development. Remind your friend that God says we must always obey Him above men (Acts 5:29). If there is ever a conflict between what God desires of us and what our family members tell us, we must yield in obedience to God—even if it leads to disruption in the family (see Matthew 10:35-39). It may be that God will use such conflict to bring other members in the family to Himself.

Bibliography

Ankerberg, John, and John Weldon. *Protestants and Catholics: Do They Now Agree?* Eugene, OR: Harvest House Publishers, 1995.

———. *The Facts on Roman Catholicism.* Eugene, OR: Harvest House Publishers, 1994.

Armstrong, John, ed. *Roman Catholicism: Evangelical Protestants Analyze What Divides and Unites Us.* Chicago: Moody Press, 1994.

Berkhof, Louis. *Manual of Christian Doctrine.* Grand Rapids, MI: William B. Eerdmans, 1983.

The Bible Knowledge Commentary: New Testament. John F. Walvoord and Roy B. Zuck, eds. Wheaton, IL: Victor Books, 1983.

The Bible Knowledge Commentary: Old Testament. John F. Walvoord and Roy B. Zuck, eds. Wheaton, IL: Victor Books, 1985.

Broderick, Robert. *The Catholic Encyclopedia.* Huntington, IN: Our Sunday Visitor, 1976.

Bruce, F.F. *The Books and the Parchments.* London: Pickering and Inglis, 1950.

Calvin, John. *Institutes of the Christian Religion.* Philadelphia, PA: Westminster, 1960.

The Canons and Decrees of the Council of Trent. H.J. Schroeder, O.P., trans. Rockford, IL: Tan Books and Publishers, 1978.

Catechism of the Catholic Church. New York, NY: Doubleday, 1994.

The Concise Evangelical Dictionary of Theology. Walter A. Elwell, ed. Grand Rapids, MI: Baker Book House, 1991.

Denzinger, Henry. *The Sources of Catholic Dogma.* St. Louis, MO: B. Herder Book Company, 1957.

Elwell, Walter A., ed. *Topical Analysis of the Bible.* Grand Rapids, MI: Baker Book House, 1991.

Erickson, Millard J. *Christian Theology.* Grand Rapids, MI: Baker Book House, 1985.

The Essential Catholic Handbook: A Summary of Beliefs, Practices, and Prayers. Liguori, MO: Liguori, 1997.

Geisler, Norman, and Thomas Howe. *When Critics Ask: A Popular Handbook on Bible Difficulties.* Wheaton, IL: Victor Books, 1992.

———, and Ralph MacKenzie. *Roman Catholics and Evangelicals: Agreements and Differences.* Grand Rapids, MI: Baker Book House, 1995.

———, and William Nix. *A General Introduction to the Bible.* Chicago, IL: Moody Press, 1978.

———, and Ron Rhodes. *When Cultists Ask.* Grand Rapids, MI: Baker Book House, 1997.

Green, Michael. *The Second Epistle of Peter and the Epistle of Jude.* Grand Rapids, MI: Eerdmans, 1968.

Hahn, Scott, and Kimberly. *Rome Sweet Home: Our Journey to Catholicism.* San Francisco, CA: Ignatius Press, 1993.

Hardon, John A. *Pocket Catholic Dictionary.* New York: Doubleday, 1966.

Johnson, S. Lewis. "Mary, the Saints, and Sacerdotalism." *Roman Catholicism: Evangelical Protestants Analyze What Divides and Unites Us.* Chicago: Moody Press, 1994.

Keating, Karl. *Catholicism and Fundamentalism: The Attack on "Romanism" by "Bible Christians."* San Francisco, CA: Ignatius Press, 1988.

Kreeft, Peter. *Fundamentals of the Faith.* San Francisco: Ignatius Press, 1988.

———, and Ronald Tacelli. *Handbook of Christian Apologetics.* Downers Grove, IL: InterVarsity Press, 1994.

Lane, William L. *The Gospel of Mark.* Grand Rapids, MI: Eerdmans, 1974.

Lightner, Robert. *Evangelical Theology: A Survey and Review.* Grand Rapids, MI: Baker Book House, 1986.

Liguoiri, St. Alphonsus. *The Glories of Mary.* Brooklyn, NY: The Redemptorist Fathers, 1931.

McCarthy, James G. *Conversations with Catholics: Catholic Tradition in Light of Biblical Truth.* Eugene, OR: Harvest House Publishers, 1997.

———. *The Gospel According to Rome: Comparing Catholic Tradition and the Word of God.* Eugene, OR: Harvest House Publishers, 1997.

Miller, Elliot, and Ken Samples. *The Cult of the Virgin.* Grand Rapids, MI: Baker, 1992.

Milne, Bruce. *Know the Truth.* Downers Grove, IL: InterVarsity Press, 1982.

Miraville, Mark. *Mark: Coredemptrix, Mediatrix, Advocate* Santa Barbara, CA: Queenship Publishing Company, 1993.

Ott, Ludwig. *Fundamentals of Catholic Dogma.* Rockford, IL: Tan Books and Publishers, 1974.

Packer, J.I. *Knowing Christianity.* Wheaton, IL: Harold Shaw Publishers, 1995.

Premm, Matthias. *Dogmatic Theology for the Laity.* Rockford, IL: Tan Books, 1967.

Rhodes, Ron. *Christ Before the Manger: The Life and Times of the Preincarnate Christ.* Grand Rapids, MI: Baker Book House, 1992.

————. *The Complete Book of Bible Answers.* Eugene, OR: Harvest House Publishers, 1997.

————. *Heaven: The Undiscovered Country—Exploring the Wonder of the Afterlife.* Eugene, OR: Harvest House Publishers, 1996.

————. *The Heart of Christianity: What It Means to Believe in Jesus.* Eugene, OR: Harvest House Publishers, 1996.

Ryrie, Charles C. *A Survey of Bible Doctrine.* Chicago: Moody Press, 1980.

————. *Basic Theology.* Wheaton, IL: Victor Books, 1986.

————. *Balancing the Christian Life.* Chicago: Moody Press, 1969.

Surprised by Truth. Patrick Madrid, ed. San Diego, CA: Basilica Press, 1994.

White, James R. *Mary—Another Redeemer?* Minneapolis, MN: Bethany House Publishers, 1998.

————. *The Roman Catholic Controversy: Catholics and Protestants—Do the Differences Still Matter?* Minneapolis, MN: Bethany House Publishers, 1996.

The Zondervan NIV Bible Commentary: New Testament. Kenneth L. Barker and John Kohlenberger III, eds. Vol. 2. Grand Rapids, MI: Zondervan Publishing House, 1994.

The Zondervan NIV Bible Commentary: Old Testament. Kenneth L. Barker and John Kohlenberger III, eds. Vol. 1. Grand Rapids, MI: Zondervan Publishing House, 1994.

Notes

Chapter 1—The Apocryphal Books Are Helpful Historically, But They Do Not Belong in the Bible

1. See Ron Rhodes, *The Complete Book of Bible Answers* (Eugene, OR: Harvest House Publishers, 1997), pp. 30-32.
2. Norman Geisler and Ralph MacKenzie, *Roman Catholics and Evangelicals: Agreements and Differences* (Grand Rapids, MI: Baker Book House, 1995), pp. 159-60.
3. Geisler and McKenzie, p. 162.
4. Geisler and McKenzie, p. 162.
5. Athanasius, "Letter 39," in Philip Schaff and Henry Wace, eds., *Nicene and Post-Nicene Fathers,* vol. 4: *Athanasius,* (Grand Rapids, MI: Eerdmans, 1978), pp. 551-52.
6. Cited in Everett F. Harrison, "The Importance of the Septuagint for Biblical Studies," *Bibliotheca Sacra,* electronic media, Logos Software.
7. W. Graham Scroggie, *A Guide to the Gospels* (Old Tappan, NJ: Revell, n.d.), p. 267.
8. Geisler and McKenzie, p. 162.
9. Geisler and McKenzie, p. 163.
10. Robert Jamieson, A.R. Fausset, and David Brown, *Commentary: Critical and Explanatory, on the Whole Bible,* electronic media, Accordance Software.

Chapter 2—The Bible Alone Is Authoritative, Not Tradition

1. Peter Kreeft, *Fundamentals of the Faith* (San Francisco: Ignatius Press, 1988), pp. 274-75.
2. John O'Brien, cited in James R. White, *The Roman Catholic Controversy* (Minneapolis: Bethany House Publishers, 1996), p. 92.
3. Norman Geisler and William Nix, *A General Introduction to the Bible* (Chicago: Moody Press, 1978), p. 28.
4. Norman Geisler and Ralph MacKenzie, *Roman Catholics and Evangelicals: Agreements and Differences* (Grand Rapids, MI: Baker Book House, 1995), p. 173.
5. F.F. Bruce, *The Books and the Parchments* (London: Pickering and Inglis, 1950), p. 111.
6. Geisler and McKenzie, p. 184.
7. White, p. 71.
8. Geisler and McKenzie, p. 196.

9. Kenneth L. Barker and John Kohlenberger III, eds., *Zondervan NIV Bible Commentary* (Grand Rapids, MI: Zondervan Publishing House, 1994), p. 16.
10. James McCarthy, *Conversations with Catholics* (Eugene, OR: Harvest House, 1997), pp. 132-33.
11. "Apostolic Tradition," Catholic Answers Home Page, copyright 1996.
12. *This Rock,* August 1992, p. 23.

Chapter 3—Peter Was a Great Apostle, But He Was Not the First Pope

1. E. Schuyler English, "Was St. Peter Ever in Rome?" *Bibliotheca Sacra,* CD, Logos Software.
2. James R. White, *The Roman Catholic Controversy* (Minneapolis: Bethany House, 1996), p. 109.
3. White, p. 110.
4. See White, p. 110.
5. William L. Lane, *The Gospel of Mark* (Grand Rapids, MI: Eerdmans, 1974), p. 134.
6. James White argues this in his book, *The Roman Catholic Controversy,* p. 117.
7. Norman Geisler and Ron Rhodes, *When Cultists Ask* (Grand Rapids, MI: Baker, 1998), p. 192.

Chapter 4—The Pope, the Bishops, and the Magisterium Are Fallible

1. *Catechism of the Catholic Church* (New York: Doubleday, 1994), p. 254.
2. *Catechism of the Catholic Church,* p. 249.
3. Henry Denzinger, *The Sources of Catholic Dogma,* electronic media, Harmony Media Inc.
4. Denzinger, *The Sources of Catholic Dogma.*
5. *The Essential Catholic Handbook* (Liguori, MO: Liguori, 1997), p. 23.
6. Hardon, John A., *Pocket Catholic Dictionary* (New York: Doubleday, 1966), p. 195.
7. *The Essential Catholic Handbook,* pp. 132-33.
8. *The Essential Catholic Handbook,* pp. 132-33.
9. See Norman Geisler and Ralph MacKenzie, *Roman Catholics and Evangelicals: Agreements and Differences* (Grand Rapids, MI: Baker Book House, 1995), p. 218.
10. See *Christian Moral Principles,* chapter 36: "A Critical Examination of Radical Theological Dissent—Some Examples of Alleged Errors in Catholic Teaching," electronic media, Harmony Media Inc.
11. *Christian Moral Principles.* See also Geisler and McKenzie, p. 219.
12. *Oxford Dictionary of the Christian Church* (Oxford: Oxford University Press, 1983), p. 66.
13. Geisler and McKenzie, p. 217.
14. Norman Geisler and Ron Rhodes, *When Cultists Ask* (Grand Rapids, MI: Baker, 1998), p. 115.
15. Michael Green, *The Second Epistle of Peter and the Epistle of Jude* (Grand Rapids, MI: Eerdmans, 1968), p. 159.
16. Geisler and McKenzie, p. 178.
17. James McCarthy, *The Gospel According to Rome* (Eugene, OR: Harvest House, 1995), pp. 263-280.
18. Craig S. Keener, *The IVP Bible Background Commentary* (Downers Grove, IL: InterVarsity Press, 1993); electronic media, Logos Software.
19. John F. Walvoord and Roy Zuck, eds., *The Bible Knowledge Commentary,* Parson's Technology.

Chapter 5—Mary Was the Mother of Jesus, Nothing More

1. See James McCarthy, *The Gospel According to Rome* (Eugene: Harvest House, 1995), p. 192.
2. Hardon, John A., *Pocket Catholic Dictionary* (New York: Doubleday, 1966), p. 272.
3. *Catechism of the Catholic Church* (New York: Doubleday, 1994), p. 142.
4. Mark Miraville, *Mary: Coredemptrix, Mediatrix, Advocate* (Santa Barbara, CA: Queenship Publishing Company, 1993), pp. xv-xvi.
5. St. Alphonsus Liguoiri, *The Glories of Mary* (Brooklyn, NY: The Redemptorist Fathers, 1931), p. 26, emphasis added.
6. Hardon, *Pocket Dictionary,* p. 32.
7. See *The Essential Catholic Handbook: A Summary of Beliefs, Practices, and Prayers* (Liguori, MO: Liguori, 1997), p. 168.
8. Kenneth R. Samples, "Apparitions of the Virgin Mary—A Protestant Look at a Catholic Phenomenon: Part Two," *Christian Research Journal,* Spring 1991, on-line electronic version.
9. *Bibliotheca Sacra* (Dallas, TX: Dallas Theological Seminary, 1955), Logos Software, insert added.
10. James White, *Mary—Another Redeemer?* (Minneapolis: Bethany, 1998), p. 25.
11. Elliot Miller and Ken Samples, *The Cult of the Virgin* (Grand Rapids, MI: Baker, 1992), p. 51.
12. See Miller and Samples, p. 23.
13. See Robert Jamieson, A.R. Fausset, and David Brown, *Commentary: Critical and Explanatory, on the Whole Bible,* electronic media, Accordance Software.

14. Lutwig Ott, *Fundamentals of Catholic Dogma* (Rockford, IL: Tan Books, 1974), p. 208.

15. S. Lewis Johnson, "Mary, the Saints, and Sacerdotalism," *Roman Catholicism: Evangelical Protestants Analyze What Divides and Unites Us* (Chicago: Moody Press, 1994), p. 124.

Chapter 6—Justification Is Instantaneous, Once-for-all, and Entirely by Grace

1. Wayne Grudem, *Systematic Theology: An Introduction to Biblical Doctrine* (Grand Rapids, MI: Zondervan Publishing House, 1994), p. 723.

2. Martin Luther, cited in J.I. Packer, *Knowing Christianity* (Wheaton, IL: Harold Shaw Publishers, 1995), p. 94.

3. *Encyclopedic Dictionary of the Bible*; electronic media, Harmony Media Inc.

4. John F. Walvoord and Roy B. Zuck, eds., *The Bible Knowledge Commentary, New Testament,* (Wheaton, IL: Victor Books, 1989), p. 825.

Chapter 7—The Sacrament of the Mass Does Not Appease God

1. Council of Trent, session 22, "Teachings and Canons on the Most Holy Sacrifice of the Mass," canon 1.

2. John A. Hardon, *Pocket Catholic Dictionary* (New York: Image Books, 1985), p. 248.

3. *Catechism of the Catholic Church* (New York: Doubleday, 1994), p. 383.

4. Liturgy of the Eucharist, First Eucharistic Prayer, the Memorial Prayer.

5. *Catechism of the Catholic Church,* pp. 334, 336.

6. Millard Erickson, *Christian Theology* (Grand Rapids, MI: Baker Book House, 1991), p. 1121.

7. Ludwig Ott, *Fundamentals of Catholic Dogma* (Rockford, IL: Tan Books, 1960), p. 374.

8. Norman Geisler and Ralph MacKenzie, *Roman Catholics and Evangelicals: Agreements and Differences* (Grand Rapids, MI: Baker Book House, 1995), p. 262.

9. Hardon, *Pocket Dictionary,* p. 468.

10. Wayne Grudem, *Systematic Theology: An Introduction to Biblical Doctrine* (Grand Rapids, MI: Zondervan Publishing House, 1994), pp. 991-94.

11. Pope John Paul II, *Crossing the Threshold of Hope;* cited in James McCarthy, *Conversations with Catholics* (Eugene, OR: Harvest House Publishers, 1997), p. 106.

12. McCarthy, *Conversations,* p. 109.

Chapter 8—The Sacrament of Penance Does Not Absolve Sins

1. *The Essential Catholic Handbook* (Liguori, MO: Liguori, 1997), p. 30.

2. Matthias Premm, *Dogmatic Theology for the Laity* (Rockford, IL: Tan Books, 1967), p. 373.

3. *The Essential Catholic Handbook,* p. 30.

4. Ludwig Ott, *Fundamentals of Catholic Dogma* (Rockford, IL: Tan Books, 1960), p. 434.

5. Ott, *Fundamentals,* p. 423.

6. Henry Denzinger, *The Sources of Catholic Dogma,* electronic media, Harmony Media Inc.

7. *Strong's Greek Lexicon,* electronic media, BibleWorks software.

Chapter 9—There Is No Purgatory, Nor Is It Needed

1. *Catechism of the Catholic Church* (New York: Doubleday, 1994), p. 291.

2. *Catechism of the Catholic Church,* p. 411.

3. See John Ankerberg and John Weldon, *Protestants and Catholics: Do They Now Agree?* (Eugene, OR: Harvest House Publishers, 1995), p. 104.

4. Ankerberg and Weldon, p. 111.

5. Ludwig Ott, *Fundamentals of Catholic Dogma* (Rockford, IL: Tan Books, 1960), p. 317.

6. Ott, p. 483.

7. Ott, p. 483.

8. Ott, p. 484.

Chapter 10—Jesus Has Changed My Life Forever

1. *Draper's Book of Quotations for the Christian World* (Grand Rapids: Baker, 1992), p. 73.

2. *Draper's Book of Quotations,* p. 65.

3. John Blanchard, *More Gathered Gold* (Darlington, Durham, Gr. Britain: Evangelical Press, 1986).

4. *Draper's Book of Quotations,* p. 66.

5. *Draper's Book of Quotations,* p. 66.

6. Blanchard, *More Gathered Gold.*

7. Blanchard, *More Gathered Gold.*

8. Walter Martin, "The Do's and Don'ts of Witnessing to Cultists," *Christian Research Newsletter,* January-February 1992, p. 4.